The Book of SAMPLERS

MARGUERITE FAWDRY
DEBORAH BROWN

LUTTERWORTH PRESS
Guildford & London

Produced by Cameron & Tayleur (Books) Limited
25 Lloyd Baker Street, London WC1X 9AT
Published by Lutterworth Press, Luke House,
Farnham Road, Guildford, Surrey GU1 4XD

Set by Input Typesetting Limited, Quadrant House,
Durnsford Road, London SW19.
Reproduction by Gateway Platemakers Limited, 1 Pardon Street, London EC1.
Printed and bound by Fabrieken Brepols n.v., Turnhout, Belgium.

First published 1980.
Printed and bound in Belgium.

ISBN 0 7188 2483 0

Designed by Ian Cameron and Mrinalini Srivastava
House editor: Mrinalini Srivastava
Copy editor: Norman Kolpas
American picture research: Bobbie Crosby
English picture research: Philippa Lewis, Bettina Tayleur

Title page. Canvas stitch sampler made by
Sarah Windrum as a demonstration piece
for teaching the craft of canvas work to
beginners. The stitches include tent, cross,
upright cross, kelim, brick; mosaic (four
variations including chequer), bargello,
Smyrna, Algerian eye, small herringbone,
jacquard, Moorish, and Gobelin (three
types – upright, oblique and encroaching).

Frontispiece. Modern sampler, worked by
Gloria Eide to record her engagement on
16th September 1977. Petit point, tent and
cross stitch worked on a fine mesh canvas.

This Italian band of embroidery has delightful versions of 'Boxers' as Cupids repeated
along its length. Late 16th or early
17th-century, double running stitch in silk
on plain weave linen, 2¼in. deep.

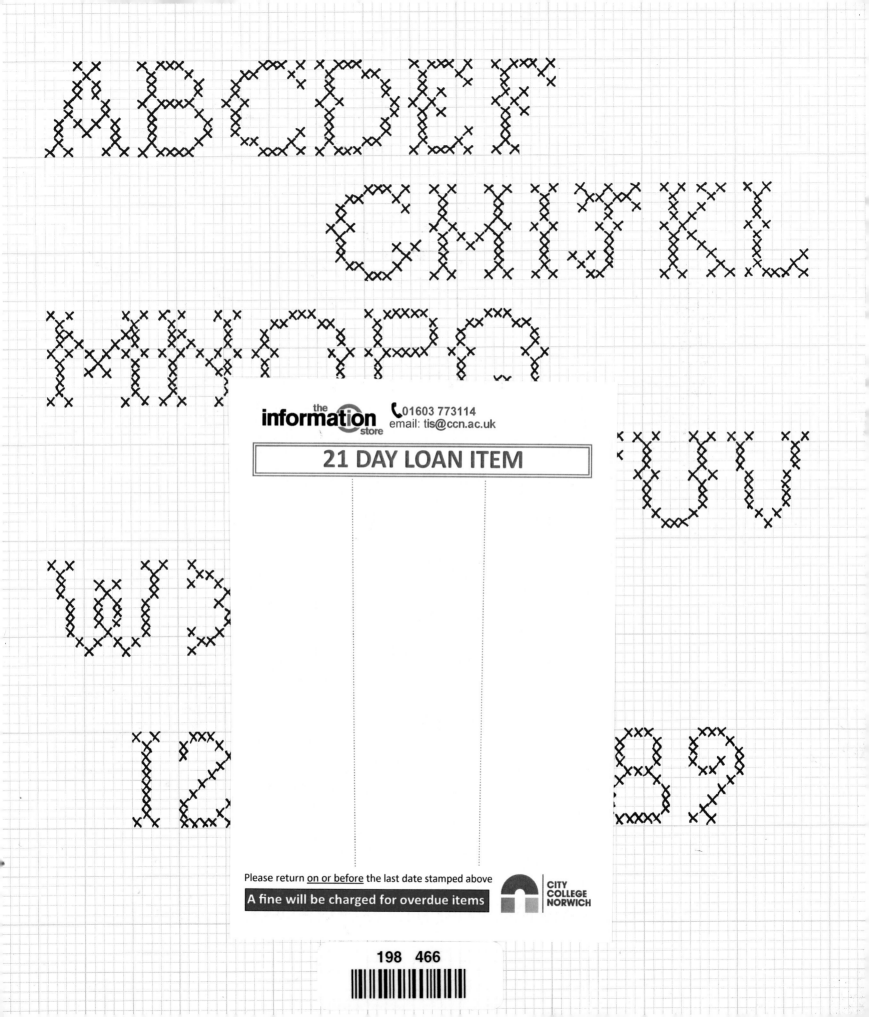

ABCDEF
GHIJKL
MNOPQ
UV
W3
12
89

Contents

Introduction

What is a sampler? The immediate image that comes to mind is a pretty, framed, embroidered picture with colourful flowers, animals, a pious verse, alphabets and probably the name and age of the little embroideress together with the date she finished her work. Most people know of samplers from seeing them hanging on a grandmother's wall or in bric-à-brac shops; more recently, samplers have appeared in up-market antique shops and sales rooms specializing in Victoriana, following a revival of interest in this once despised period of decorative arts. Ladies of older generations may also associate the term sampler with needlework exercises done at school when they struggled with buttonholes and complicated seams on tiny scraps of fabric. But for most people a sampler is a product of the Victorian age, charming but useless, a part of the clutter of fancy work with which ladies filled their time, producing such items as crepe paper splash-backs for the washstand and fly rests, which were mobiles hung from the ceiling to attract the flies and encourage them to settle rather than buzzing around your head.

Few people realize that samplers have been made for several centuries, that they are known not only in most European countries but also in Asia, and that there is a good deal of evidence to show that they were known in antiquity too. It is, in fact, only in the 19th century that the sampler became purely decorative—a showpiece to hang on the parlour wall—and lost its former role as a record of stitches and patterns.

It is difficult to separate the history of the sampler from that of embroidery —a craft whose origins are lost in history. In the summer of 1978 the British Museum put on show two extraordinary finds. At first sight they looked just like soft toys, discarded playthings from the bottom of any modern toy cupboard. They were swans, about a foot long, made of different-coloured felts and stuffed with deer hair. The wings and tail feathers were outlined in dark stitching, and small wooden pins inserted in their feet stood them upright. The exhibit label offered the following information:

High Altai, barrow 5. Excavations S. I. Rudenko 1949. Early nomadic culture, 5th and 4th centuries BC.

These objects had been preserved for nearly two and a half thousand years in the frozen depths of a Siberian burial chamber . By a miracle of nature, some of the most ancient examples of needlework in the world looked as though they could have been made yesterday by any mother with a few scraps of fabric and a little time on her hands.

The Hermitage Museum in Leningrad had sent the swans to London as part of an extraordinary array of precious objects excavated from Siberia in the 18th century and originally belonging to the collection of Peter the Great. The exhibition also included more recently discovered treasures—bronze and copper horse trappings, knives, daggers, mirrors—all stylishly decorated with lively animal figures. Yet it was the wood, leather, fur and textile objects that most compelled attention. In the permanently frozen ground, they had retained their original shape and bright colours. There were saddle-cloths, covered with richly embroidered Chinese silk or decorated with appliqués of coloured felt and fine leather; bootees trimmed with spirals of tiny beads and metal-wrapped thread; socks and stockings; the remains of a hairnet, woven in dark red wool; a large man's shirt; a child's tiny fur coat; and the felt swans.

Twenty-five centuries ago the women of these Siberian tribes had sat patiently to fashion the warm, comfortable garments necessary for survival in a harsh, inhospitable climate. The accidental preservation of these textile objects is of paramount importance, because, by the very nature of fabric, specimens of early needlework were usually lost to posterity. Although count-less women spent the greater part of their lives spinning, weaving, sewing and embroidering, little of this work survives from before the 10th century AD. To gather information on early sewing and embroidery techniques, we have to rely mostly on documentary evidence from frescoes and sculptures.

Very early in human development, the need to produce clothes to keep out the cold appears to have combined with the desire to produce patterns and embellishments on skins and textiles with needle and thread. Sewing needles were among the earliest tools used by human beings. In prehistoric sites archaeologists have found needles made from animal bones, wood, ivory, stone, long stout thorns, and, later, from bronze and iron. These tools were not used merely to join seams but also to ornament the whole garment. It is quite probable that the poor quality of early textiles required some technique to strengthen them; the application of stitched patterns would have had this effect. In the earliest known examples of embroidery, the thread used was made of wool, flax or cotton. Wool was, of course, the first of these; flax, which gave linen thread, was used by more advanced civiliz-ations, such as that of ancient Egypt. Cotton was common in the East. And as early as 1200 BC, silk was developed in China, from where it travelled to Persia and India.

The Roman historian Pliny the Elder, who died in AD 79, tells us: 'Babylon devoted itself to the manufacture of embroideries of various colours, called Babylonian embroidery; while Alexandria invented the art of weaving stuffs with many threads, which were called brocades.' Sculpted figures in stone monuments are today the only evidence we have of the splendid golden embroideries of Babylon. But those of Alexandria have, by another quirk of nature, been preserved in the dry sand of the burial grounds of ancient Egypt.

Mummies were bound with strips of linen, a material that was regarded as very precious because the flax it was made from was a gift from the goddess Isis. To give a mummy a more even shape, odd bits of material—clothing or curtain hangings—were rolled up and stuffed round its neck. In this way many early examples of embroidery technique were preserved. The high skill reached by Egyptian textile workers had already been noted in antiquity. Herodotus described a garment that belonged to Amasis, King of Egypt: 'It was of linen ornamented with numerous figures of animals, worked in gold and cotton. Each thread of the corselet was worthy of admiration.'

When the custom of mummification ceased in Egypt, people were dressed for burial in their everyday clothes; then they were wrapped up in any

A piece of Coptic embroidery with early Christian symbols worked in darning stitch. Silk on linen, AD 400-500.

convenient length of material and strapped to a wooden board. The bodies were buried in the dry, sandy soil, often in several layers. There they remained until 19th and 20th century archaeologists discovered them, classified and catalogued their garments, socks, fragments of tunics, even little dolls' dresses, and displayed them in museums throughout the world.

It is from the Coptic Church in Egypt that the earliest embroidered symbols of the Christian faith have come down to us, presaging the great flowering of ecclesiastical art in the Middle Ages. European textiles generally progressed during the Roman period. When St Augustine reached Kent in 597, it is said he carried a great banner emblazoned with the figure of Christ. It has even been suggested that the embroidery done much later in England, during the 17th and 18th centuries, bore a strong resemblance to Egyptian works from the time of Julius Caesar—an indication that these traditional designs were a legacy of Roman rule. But, unfortunately, there is no surviving specimen of embroidery done in Roman Britain.

Another theory claims that embroidery was carried to Britain by captive women who were brought over from southern Europe during the Anglo-Saxon and Danish invasions. There is no doubt that embroidery flourished under Saxon rule. Anglo-Saxon women's craftsmanship was famous throughout Europe. Few examples survive, but there is considerable written evidence. In a poem composed in the 7th century, St Aldhelm, scholar, Abbot of Malmesbury and later Bishop of Sherborne, greatly praised the tapestry work and embroidery done by the women of his time. In the seclusion of their convents, 'nuns with their needles wrote histories also, that of Christ, his passion, as other scripture stories to adorn their houses,' wrote an early chronicler of the Christian Church. Nuns were not alone in this passion for embroidery. In the courts of kings and the households of the well-to-do, ladies devoted their time to the craft. William of Malmesbury described Edgithea, wife of Edward the Confessor, as a perfect mistress of her needle. She embroidered the mantle worn by the king at his coronation. Nevertheless, the greatest impetus came from the convents and the main output of embroidery was, not surprisingly, ecclesiastical.

Queen Matilda, wife of William the Conqueror, extended her patronage to numerous churches and her gifts included her own work and that of professional embroiderers. The Holy Trinity Church at Caen in Normandy, for example, received her gold embroidered mantle, which was later made into a cape. But Queen Matilda's name is largely, and probably erroneously, associated with the Bayeux Tapestry. Opinions about this differ, and some authors suggest that the Matilda of the tapestry was not the wife of the Conqueror but Empress Matilda, the grand-daughter of William the Conqueror and the wife of Henry V, Emperor of Germany, and later of Geoffrey of Anjou. On the other hand, A. F. Kendrick maintains in his book *English Needlework*, that the Bayeux Tapestry was made by people who must have been Norman themselves and who favoured the conquest. He argues that to believe the work was embroidered between fifty and a hundred years after the event is to endow its makers with a profound historic sense and a phenomenal knowledge of local detail.

The argument in no way alters the historical value of the Bayeux work. To be accurate, this unique specimen should be described as an embroidery, not a tapestry, and it was probably worked over a long period. A piece of linen more than 230 feet long and 20 inches wide, it records the accession of Edward the Confessor to the downfall of Harold, in an amazing cavalcade of armoured characters, ships, horses and weapons. No less than 1255 figures appear on the cloth, and its importance as a social and historical document exceeds its intrinsic value as a piece of embroidery. Indeed, the standard of workmanship cannot be held to represent the finest of the period. Earlier work of greater quality survives. The embroiderers, working with wool, obviously found that laid and couched work combined with outline stitches was a very suitable technique for rapidly executing a series of vivid scenes.

The splendid medieval vestments and altar cloths now preserved in French, Italian and English churches were often the work of English nuns between the 12th and 14th centuries, when English needlework was at its height. The words *Opus Anglicanum*, used in church archives to describe these early vestments, not only denoted their country of origin but were also regarded as a testimonial certificate to the excellence of the workmanship. It seems that many nuns enjoyed their sewing more than reading pious books or attending devotions; official reprimands survive which decree that no nun should absent herself from divine service for the sake of her silk work.

The two hundred years during which *Opus Anglicanum* won the envy and admiration of Europe coincided with a great tide of excellence in other arts. Illuminators, workers in wood and in metal, in stone and in ivory, left works of great skill and inventiveness. The work of English artists and embroiderers was sought throughout Europe. Pope Innocent IV wrote in 1246: 'England is our garden of delight, . . . it is an inexhaustible well, wherein there is great abundance, from whence much may be extracted.' He contacted several Cistercian monasteries in England, requesting them to send to him *Opus Anglicanum* vestments.

The popularity of their embroidery provided convents with a considerable source of income. Evidence shows, however, that some poorer religious houses accepted too many orders, and nuns complained of overwork. The report of a visit to Eastbourne in 1441 quotes the nuns as saying that 'the

Portion of the Bayeux Tapestry. It shows Harold, leader of the English, riding to Bosham, arriving at church, and then eating a meal with his followers.

Prioress compels her Sisters to work continually like hired workwomen, and they receive nothing for their own use from their work, but the Prioress takes the whole lot.' However, compared with the tough outside world, life within the protective walls of one of the richer nunneries was not excessively hard. Women of intellect could learn to read and write—rare accomplishments in those days. Others could develop their talents for teaching, medicine, nursing or administration. And many could find in sewing and embroidery a satisfying outlet for their artistic gifts.

Much of the embroidery called for co-operative work because of the size, scope and complexity of the projects. In 1271, for example, an altar frontal was given to Westminster Abbey. It took four women four years to complete. All such works are characterized by an astonishing evenness and fineness of stitch. The faces of the characters depicted were worked in split stitch, to produce a raised effect.

During the 15th century, English embroidery began to decline. Troubles at home and abroad pervaded the later Middle Ages and affected artists and craftsmen. The Black Death and the Hundred Years War with France brought economic and social distress. Britain, like the rest of Europe, fell into a general state of unrest.

The stitchery of this time, although still elaborate and sumptuous, lacked the distinctiveness and creative drive evident in earlier works. This decline did not come suddenly. It was reinforced by the disbanding of the old craft guilds and particularly by the dissolution of the monasteries under Henry VIII in 1536. In troubled times, the convents had remained islands of peace in which rich embroideries were still produced. But even the final closure of religious houses did not entirely eclipse good embroidery. The many surviving portraits of Henry VIII show him wearing clothes ablaze with elaborate

Women sewing, an early woodcut.

Opposite, left. Example of *Opus Anglicanum* – panel from a 13th-century cope depicting The Coronation of The Virgin.

stitchery. Nevertheless, English embroidery lost its unique supremacy, and other styles and influences were brought to Britain from continental Europe.

It is sad to realize how few of the costly, medieval embroideries of the *Opus Anglicanum* period have survived the onslaught of time and human destruction. Important church dignitaries were usually buried in their albs and copes; altar-cloths were sometimes cut up to serve as wrappings for holy relics, or they were burnt to recover the gold thread and jewels with which

Portrait of Henry VIII by an unknown artist, *c*1542.

Book cover said to have been worked by Elizabeth I when she was eleven years old. It covered her translation from French of *The Mirroir or Glasse of the Synnefull Soule*. She gave the book to her stepmother, Katherine Parr, as a New Year's gift 'on the last day of the yeare, 1544'. Ornamental filigree work in gold and silver wire on blue corded silk with the initials K.P. in the middle of each cover.

they were encrusted. After Henry VIII's break with the Church of Rome, some ecclesiastical embroideries were even confiscated and converted to bedspreads or tablecloths.

All over Europe, wherever the forces of the Reformation triumphed, monasteries and convents were closed and their inmates compelled to seek secular outlets for their skills. As a result, throughout the 16th century, a more gracious way of living evolved, fostered by servants who had once sought only to serve God. The huge, draughty fortress castles of the Middle Ages gave way to more graceful manor houses surrounded by formal gardens. Between low, clipped hedges, parterres of flowers grew where once there had been only plots of cabbages or onions. The ladies of the household used their skill with the needle to embellish curtains, bed-hangings, pillows and cushions with a profusion of leaves, flowers and intricate designs.

These luxuries were not enjoyed by the nobility alone in Tudor England. William Harrison wrote in 1577, in his *Chronicles of England*, 'In the houses

Princess Elizabeth aged 13½ by an unknown artist.

Elizabethan coverlet worked in silks and plaited gold thread in long and short stitch.

Opposite, above. Elizabethan blackwork linen head-dress embroidered in black silk and trimmed with bobbin lace.

Opposite, below. Cushion cover worked by Mary, Queen of Scots, Her cypher is surrounded with the flowers of the three countries of which she considered she was, or had been, Queen: lily for France, rose for England and thistle for Scotland.

14

of knights and gentlemen merchantmen and some other wealthy citizens, it is no so geson [rare] to behold generally their great provision of tapestry, Turkey work . . . and fine linen. Many farmers garnish . . . their beds with tapestry and fine silk hangings and their tables with carpets and drapery . . . whereby the wealth of the country . . . doth infinitely appear.' Among women, this greater prosperity also fostered a taste for expensive clothes. One glance at Queen Elizabeth's portraits reveals the intricacy and magnificence of contemporary embroidery; her gowns were ablaze with it. Her huge wardrobe—over 2,000 dresses—must have been a compensation for her dreary childhood: after the loss of favour and subsequent death of her mother, Anne Boleyn, she was so neglected that her governess had to plead with the king to get clothing for her. 'She hath neither gown or kirtle,' wrote Lady Bryan, 'nor petticoat, nor no manner of linen, nor foresmocks, nor kerchiefs, nor rails, nor body stitchets, nor handkerchiefs, nor sleeves, nor muffler, nor biggens.'

As she grew older, Princess Elizabeth's position at court improved. She received a wide-ranging education in foreign languages, some Latin, music, dancing—and needlework. Several items worked by her hands still exist, notably a book cover that she may have given her stepmother, Katherine Parr, and eighteen pieces of baby linen made for her half-sister, Queen Mary.

But it is doubtful whether Princess Elizabeth was as skilled in the art of embroidery as the other Mary, her cousin, the future Queen of Scots. As befitted a future Queen of France, Mary had been carefully trained in all the courtly accomplishments of her time. We are told that she sang very well, attuning her voice to the lute, which she played prettily; that she danced excellently; and that she devoted great attention to the study of European languages. Her future mother-in-law, Catherine de Medici, herself an enthusiastic needlewoman, made sure that Mary was taught needlework. The skill was a source of pleasure and recreation to Mary throughout her life. During the long years of her captivity in England, she worked—together with the wife of her jailor, Elizabeth Countess of Shrewsbury—magnificent sets of bed-hangings that today epitomize the splendour of Elizabethan embroidery.

After the execution of Mary Queen of Scots, every particle of her clothing and possessions was burnt, so that no relic might remain around which a cult could grow. Her hated jailor, Sir Amyas Paulet, reported that he had found 'a box full of abominable trash with bands of all sorts, pictures in silks and some agnus dei.'

Royal needlewomen were not alone in the delight they took in fine sewing. The writer Barnabe Riche, in his tale 'Of Phylotus and Emilia', described the pastimes of a rich man's wife: 'Now when she had dined, then she might go seke out her examplers, whiche in a quaife, whiche in a caule, whiche in a handcarcheef; what lace would doe nexte to edge it, what seame, what stitche, what cutte, what garde; and to sitte her doune and take it forthe by little and little, and thus with her needle to passe the afternoon with devising of things for her owne wearynge.'

Like that rich man's wife, it is time for us, too, to seek out our examplers, which is to say, samplers. We have now reached the period in embroidery that yielded the first surviving sampler.

EARLY SAMPLERS

Embroidered was he, as it were a meade
All full of freshe flourés white and rede.

The Young Squire in
The Canterbury Tales
(Geoffrey Chaucer, 1477)

Our quest for samplers has brought us to the 16th century and the first written records of samplers. The earliest reference is dated 1502: Elizabeth of York's account book shows that eight pennies were charged to her by Thomas Fissch for an 'elne of lynnyn cloth for a sampler', the English elne or ell measuring about 44 inches. The will of Margaret Thomson, made at Freston in Holland, Lincolnshire in 1546, states that 'I gyve to Alys Pynchebeck my sister's daughter my sawmpler with semes.' It is not quite certain what 'with semes' means, but it is probable that the piece consisted of various methods for joining seams: in Tudor times, much fine work went into beautifying the 'open seams' rendered necessary by very narrow looms. And a list of Edward VI of England's possessions, dated 1552, included twelve samplers and 'one samplar of Normandie canvas wrought with green and black silk.'

In some European countries, such as Spain, there is also contemporary written evidence of samplers. An inventory of the Queen of Spain's household, dated 1509, lists fifty samplers, some worked in silk, others in gold thread. A picture dating from the 14th century, kept in the Church of San Francisco in Villafranca del Panades (Barcelona), represents seven young women, the Virgin Mary among them; they show their needlework, which looks suspiciously like samplers, to an older woman.

It seems very strange that no earlier English sampler should have survived than that of Jane Bostocke, worked in 1598. The piece is now kept in the Victoria and Albert Museum, in London, which houses one of the most important sampler collections of Europe. Jane's sampler is not a picture enclosed in a border, but a strip of unbleached linen measuring 43 by 38 cm. It is inscribed, 'Jane Bostocke 1598' and further down, 'Alice Lee was borne the 23rd of November being Tuesday in the afternoone 1596'. At the top of the sampler is a dog carrying its lead, a deer, a chained bear, a little heraldic terrier and some floral motifs. All these figures are placed quite haphazardly on the cloth, and are followed by an alphabet, an inscription, a profusion of sample borders and patterns running higgledy-piggledy one after the other.

The workmanship is exquisite, with red, brown, blue and white silks as well as with some metal thread, seed pearls and black beads. The sampler displays a complex variety of stitches: back, satin, chain, ladder, buttonhole

Opposite, right. Jane Bostocke's gift sampler is the earliest surviving dated sampler: 1598. The inscription reads:
ALICE:LEE:WAS:BORNE:THE:23:OF:NOVEMBER:BEING:TUESDAY:IN:THE:AFTER:NOONE:1596

Opposite, left. Susan Nebrabi's whitework band sampler. It shows the arms of Elizabeth I in cut and drawn thread work, *c*1580-1600.

and detached button hole, coral, two-sided Italian cross, couching, speckling and French knots. We can safely assume that Jane made it for the then two-year-old Alice Lee as a present and as a record of stitches for her daughter to use later as she learned to sew.

Discovered in 1960, the sampler has the distinction of being the earliest surviving English sampler to carry a date and the name of the embroideress. But other early pieces, such as the band sampler made by Susan Nebabri, are now kept at the Museum of London. It is believed to have been made between 1580 and 1600, but there is no certainty about the date. There are also three early samplers in the Carew Pole Collection. One has three large patterns worked on it, mainly in tent stitch, along with five or six smaller motifs. The colours used are green and black silk, sewn in cross stitch and back stitch. The running scroll border, with columbines and a lozenge design of linked hexagons, is remarkably similar to the patterns worked on a set of six pillow covers still preserved at Antony House, Torpoint, Cornwall, the home of the Carew Pole family. Because the same lozenge pattern also occurs on a cushion cover, with a flower embroidery in colour at its centre, it is likely that the small piece was done to work out and practise the design before starting the pillow covers.

It is difficult to understand why no earlier samplers have survived—especially since much more ancient examples of embroidered garments or ecclesiastical vestments, which must have endured considerably more wear and tear than a sampler, still remain for us to study. Furthermore, early samplers were made of coarse linen, which is fairly impervious to damage by moths. It is interesting to note, for example, that early 17th-century samplers are often far better preserved than those done in Victorian times: moths and damp often played havoc with the woollen cloth or canvas on which later samplers were frequently worked. It is as though the country was purged of samplers at the time of Charles I's death.

The Puritans are unlikely to have been the authors of such destruction, as so many fine specimens of samplers date from the Commonwealth period. These God-fearing people regarded needlework as a virtuous talent in their women. The Puritans carried this skill to America, giving rise to the great tradition of American sampler-making. American samplers mingle the mainstream influences of 17th-century sampler design with the invigorating forces that the settlers found in the New World.

Despite the absence of earlier European specimens, it is still reasonable to suppose that samplers were worked in the Middle Ages. At the height of the fame of *Opus Anglicanum*, needlework must have been practised on some kind of sampler. Mention of samplers in Shakespeare's writings and in those

Blackwork cushion cover from the Carew-Pole collection.

Opposite, above. Detail for tapestry work in the Carew-Pole collection with typical Tudor flower designs.

Opposite, below. This piece of embroidery is probably not a sampler, but a cushion cover. It was worked by Mary Hulton and features the arms of James I.

of other Elizabethan poets suggest that both the word and the object were firmly entrenched in contemporary imagery. In her book *Samplers of Yesterday and Today*, Averil Colby examines the etymology of the word in great detail. 'Sampler' comes from the Latin *exemplum*, which describes anything that serves as a pattern for imitation or record. In early English texts the words *exemplar* or *exemple* are used instead of 'sampler'. There were many variants, however: *ensample, saumplerie, sawmpler, sam-cloth* and *sampleth*. In Salesbury's *A Dictionary in Englyshe and Welshe*, published in 1547, we find the spelling *siampler*, and in John Davies's *Antiquae Linguae Britannicae* are *siampl, siampler, exemplar*. And an earlier dictionary, *Lesclarissement de la Langue Francoyse*, compiled by John Palsgrave in 1530, offers the word 'sampler', defined as 'an exampler for a woman to work by'.

It is difficult to judge for certain if an early piece of embroidery was intended as a sampler or served some other purpose. There is, for example, in the Victoria and Albert Museum a small Elizabethan panel six inches square, embroidered in silk and gold thread on linen. It shows St Veronica holding the sacred napkin, surrounded by other emblems of the Passion. In the border are inscribed the words 'Ihesu Fili Dei Miserere, mei Praye for me Anne Inglebye'. Although it looks like a sampler, A. F. Kendrick, former Keeper of the Textile Collection, does not believe it is one. He thinks it may have been designed to serve as a cover for a book of devotion. Likewise, he also considers that a larger panel in the collection, with the arms of King James I enclosed by flowering plants, animals, and birds, and bearing the worker's name Mary Hulton in large letters, was probably intended as a cushion cover.

Many of the patterns on the earlier samplers resemble those found on

Early 17th-century random motifs worked in coloured silks on linen canvas in tent stitch. The motifs would then be cut out and appliquéd on bed hangings and other furnishings.

bags, purses, handkerchiefs and garments. Occasionally, too, a small panel comes down to us as a cushion or a bag, although to all appearances it would seem to have been intended primarily as a sampler. It is easy to imagine that an embroiderer having produced a piece of work originally meant as practice, might want to transform this rather pleasing sampler into a purse or some other small object. Another type of work common at the time was 'slips'—long strips of linen worked with a random selection of motifs. When finished, the slips were cut out and applied in an orderly design on some larger piece of work, such as bed-hangings, which would have been unwieldy to embroider on their own. It is, of course, difficult to distinguish between such strips, which may not have been applied to a larger piece and therefore remain intact, and genuine samplers—particularly since early samplers were almost always worked on long, narrow strips of linen. As A. F. Kendrick has written:

> Probably sampler making was not so general in the 16th century. What form the exercises of immature needleworkers took still earlier is unknown to us, and there is nothing to show whether anything corresponding to the sampler was made at all. It is uncertain, too, whether samplers first made their appearance as exercises in proficiency, as records of attainment, or as repertoires of design for future use. The sampler is an exampler or pattern, and probably it had its first beginnings as a record of designs for reference in later years.

Between the first mention of the word 'sampler' in 1502 and Jane Bostocke's sampler in 1598 there is a span of 96 years. This period encompasses the end of Henry VII's reign, all of Henry VIII's, his son Edward's, his daughter Mary's, and all but five years of Elizabeth I's. We certainly should not conclude, however, that the absence of samplers from this time means that embroidery had been neglected.

During Elizabeth's extraordinary reign, tremendous advances occurred in every sphere of life, including the minor arts. Fresh ideas and materials poured in from the New World; imports from the East, through the newly-established trading companies, exerted an enormous influence on the whole field of textiles. The influx from Europe of skilled craftsmen anxious to escape religious persecution also affected the textile field. All these factors led to improvements in technical methods and forms of expressions. Old English traditions of embroidery were not lost; they were rejuvenated and given fresh impetus. Housewives and noble ladies all used their leisure time to create beautiful embroidery on new types of fabric, using silk threads imported from the Levant. In 1561, Queen Elizabeth granted to the Broders' Company its first charter. Other European nations soon followed the example she set.

Jane Bostocke's sampler serves as a unique guide to the popular contemporary stitches and patterns. These can be compared with the few Elizabethan embroidered garments and furnishings that still exist, or with contemporary portrait paintings in which costume details show clearly.

Embroidery in black silk on white linen—blackwork—was already fashionable during the reign of Henry VIII. Its popularity continued well into the 17th century. Both men and women wore, next to their skin, a long linen shirt. Its front, together with the collar and parts of the sleeves and cuffs, was visible under the rich outer garments. To embroider these parts of the shirt was not merely elegant and decorative; it also served practical purposes, strengthening the cloth, and disguising the stains and grubbiness that inevitably resulted with the period's rather low standards of hygiene. Indeed, one cannot help wondering how these garments could ever be washed clean; contemporary laundry soap consisted of ashes and hog dung or cow dung, and their recipes for making black dyes are even more alarming, containing ingredients such as soot, vitriol, walnut shells, elder bark and lye made from ashes.

The stitch used for creating blackwork patterns has been given different names: 'Holbein', because many of the painter's sitters wore clothes ornamented in this way; 'Spanish stitch', because the introduction of this type of embroidery is often attributed to Catherine of Aragon, who came to England from Spain in 1501 to marry Prince Arthur. In Spain the tradition of Moorish geometric blackwork embroideries had existed for centuries. However, Chaucer's description of the carpenter's wife Alison, would seem to indicate that a similar type of embroidery was known in England before Catherine's arrival.

> Her smock was white; embroidery repeated
> Its pattern on the collar front and back,
> Inside and out; it was of silk and black.

For accuracy, we can call the black stitch 'double-running', because the pattern is worked over twice so that there is no wrong side to the finished work. This was important for collars and cuffs, which needed to look identical on both sides.

Double-running stitch also suited the intricate linear geometrical patterns of the early Renaissance, many of which were adapted from pattern-books designed for lace-making, or from line drawings which gave no guidance on

Miniature by Isaac Oliver of a young man c1590. The collar of his shirt shows the fashionable blackwork, with reticella trimmings on the cuffs. The knot garden in the background is typical of the period; such gardens are often echoed in contemporary embroidery – see the book cover on page 13.

how to work them with needle and thread. Printing from engraved copper plates was perfected during the latter part of Elizabeth's reign. As engraved illustrations became more widely circulated, the pattern possibilities of embroidery were enlarged. This influence is seen not only in embroidery but in lace, jewellery, wrought iron, wall paintings, plaster ceilings—and in the formal layout of Tudor knot gardens, with their sweet-smelling herbs and flowers enclosed in neatly trimmed borders. William Lawson, in his *Country Housewife's Garden*, published in 1617, gave diagrams which look just like emboidery patterns but really show how to create knot gardens. 'The number of formes, mazes, knots is so great,' he wrote, 'that I leave every housewife to herself lest I deprive her of all delight and direction. Let her view these new forms, and note this generally: that all plots are square and all are bordered about with privit, raisins, feaberries, roses, thorne, rosemary, bee flowers, isop, sage and such like.'

For the sake of convenience, the rest of this book is divided up into centuries, which, it must be admitted, is a highly artificial classification. Young girls are taught to sew by their mothers or grandmothers. Well-loved and tried patterns and stitches overlap, do not change with fashion and survive intact or in a slightly modified form through centuries. For this reason, Anne Gower's sampler, although it is assumed to have been worked in 1610, is included here among early samplers. She embroidered it in her childhood in England, but in 1628 she followed her husband, Governor Endicott, to America. She died in Salem, Massachusetts one year later but her sampler is still preserved at the Essex Institute in Salem. It consists of intricate cut and drawn thread work as well as flat whitework, and includes her name and an alphabet. It is regarded as the earliest sampler found in America.

Blackwork and whitework techniques are typical examples of the difficulty encountered when trying to draw a demarcation line between one century and another. Blackwork described as a 16th-century technique, endured well into the next century. Cut work and lace needlepoint stitches, although already popular in Elizabethan times, really belong to the 17th century.

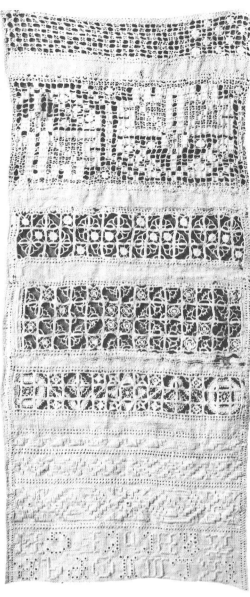

Above. Cut and drawn whitework sampler, 18 × 8in., made in England *c*1610 by Anne Gower. She brought it with her to America when she married Governor John Endecott in 1628.

Left. Designs for 'ret' and 'lozenge' knot gardens from William Lawson's *The Country House-Wifes Garden* (1617).

22

PRACTICAL-EARLY SAMPLERS

Vine and grape design. One of Jane Bostocke's repeat all-over patterns. Worked in silk on linen in double running stitch, this is an example of blackwork technique, although she uses red, green and pale brown thread as well as black.

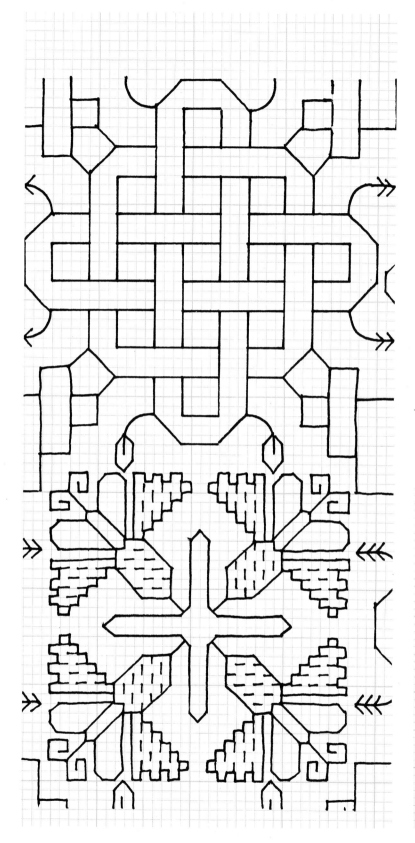

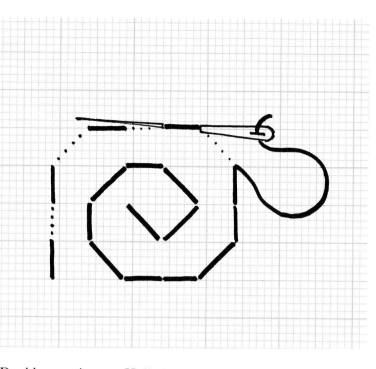

Double running or Holbein stitch. Evenly spaced running stitches are worked in one direction and filled in on the return journey.

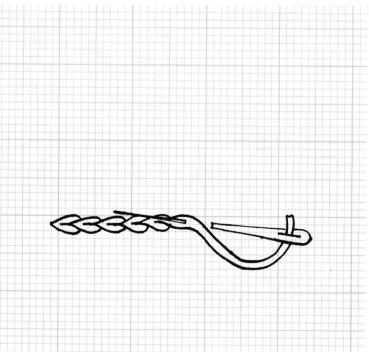

Another area of Jane Bostocke's sampler which uses the same technique as illustrated on the previous page.

Split stitch. Backstitch which pierces the thread, forming a chain. Worked left to right. This is one of the oldest known stitches. It was widely used in *Opus Anglicanum*.

THE SEVENTEENTH CENTURY

Designs for reticella from *The Needle's Excellency* (1636).

Here Practice and Invention may be free,
And as a Squirrell skips from tree to tree,
So maids may (from their Mistresses, or their Mother)
Learne to leave one worke, and to learne an other,
For here they may make choyce of which is which,
And skip from worke to worke, from stitch to stitch,
Until, in time, delightfull practice shall
(With profit) make them perfect in them all.

These lines of doggerel come from the poem *The Needle's Excellency*, by John Taylor, a Thames waterman, publican and merchant who called himself the Water Poet. The poem gave its name to the 12th edition of a book of needlework patterns published in London in 1632. The original designs, the work of Johan Sibmacher, had been published in Germany in 1597 under the title *Schön Neues Modelbuch*. The English version ran into many editions and the book has never really gone out of use: facsimile reproductions came out in Germany in 1866 and 1877, and in 1975 in the United States under the title *Baroque Charted Designs for Needlework*. Its publishers, Dover Publications, have also reproduced another early pattern book, *Renaissance Patterns for Lace, Embroidery and Needlepoint*. It was designed by Frederico Vinciolo and published in 1587 under the title *I Singolari e Nuovi Disegni*; between that date and 1658 it was reprinted many times. Under the title *A Booke of Curious and Strange Inventions, called the first part of needleworkes*, the book was published for 'the profit and delight of the gentlewomen of England', by William Barley. The patterns are described as 'many singular and fine sortes of cutworkes, raised workes, stitches and opent cutworks, verie easie to be learned by the diligent practisers that shall follow the direction contained.'

Frederico Vinciolo was employed by Catherine de Medici to make the enormous starched ruffs she had brought into fashion in Paris. Catherine also brought to France from her native Italy the art of needlepoint embroidery. At her death, she left over a thousand squares of netted embroidery worked by herself, with designs very similar to those of Vinciolo. Vinciolo's book must have been extremely important in England, judging by the strong Italian influence so clearly visible on samplers in the 16th and 17th centuries, when cut and lace work were so popular. Italian work was distinguished by attractive coloured borders, a coloured central piece, and geometrical patterns of a floral type, showing a strong Islamic influence. Other Venetian pattern books such as *La Vera Perfettione del disegno* and Parasole's *Pretiosa Gemma delle virtuose donne* greatly popularized the geometrical outlines suitable for cut and drawn work.

In 1624, *The Schole House of the Needle* appeared. Richard Shorleyker added this explanatory note to the second edition of 1632: 'Here followeth the

Designs for reticella from *The Needle's Excellency* (1636).

certaine patterns of art workes, and but once printed before. Also sundry sorts of spots, as Flowers, Birds and Fishes etc, and will fitly serve to be wrought, some with gould, some with silke, and some with crewell, or other wise at your pleasure.'

The designs and patterns found in these various books were certainly not the original inspirations of Sibmacher, Shorleyker or even Vinciolo. Most were copied from the patterns found on Oriental and Italian imported silk fabrics, which were the current rage. In a period which knew no law of copyright, these motifs and patterns were indiscriminately reproduced from one book to another. Even the works of great artists such as Dürer and Holbein were adapted to make needlework patterns.

Of course, part of the fun of sampler-making is to copy or adapt patterns or pictures that strike your fancy. At the end of the book there is a page divided in squares which is accompanied by the caption:

'I would have you knowe, that the use of these squares clothe showe how you may continue any work, Bird, Beast or Flower, into bigger or lesser proportions according as you shall see cause: as thus, if you will enlarge your patterne, divide it into squares, then rule a paper as large as you list, into what squares you will. Then looke how many holes your patterne doth containe, upon so many holes of your ruled paper drawe your patterne'.

This method still holds good. A small girl learning to sew today might enjoy enlarging tenfold one of Richard Shorleyker's birds, beasts or flowers and working it in thick wool on a large square of Binca canvas.

Another traditional method of transferring the design from the printed page to the material to be worked consisted of outlining the design with a

Design of a man killing a stag and a peacock from the 1587 French edition of Frederico di Vinciolo's *Les Singuliers et Nouveaux Pourtraicts pour Toutes Sortes d'Ouvrages de Lingerie.*

series of pinholes, through which a dark charcoal powder was shaken on the material. Pricking out the picture with pins and needles of varying thickness and then holding it up to the light probably became a favourite remembered childhood pastime. As the poet William Cowper wrote of past, happy days with his mother:

> Could Time, his flight reversed restore the hours
> When, playing with they vestures tissued flowers
> The violets, the pink, the jessamin
> I pricke'd them into paper with a pin.
>
> *On Receipt of My Mother's Picture.*

Sadly, this practice led to the loss of many old books, their pages ripped out to be used as pinprick patterns.

Another interesting characteristic of early pattern books was that they also contained pages divided into squares on which the owner of the book could draw her own patterns. This practice was the origin of pattern paper, purchased by the sheet, which did not become available until a century later. It appears, once again, that the idea originated in Germany: Johan Tobias Frölich from Augsburg is often given credit for it.

In Elizabethan times, books were still rare and precious possessions. But in time, library shelves filled and people's horizons widened. In the 17th century, animals and plants, which had previously been regarded merely as witnesses to the greatness of God, now became the object of scientific curiosity. Plants from the Old and the New World were illustrated in herbals and books on gardening. Strange animals were shown in the engravings of Edward Topsell's *The History of Four Footed Beasts*, published in 1607. Thomas Moufet's work on insects appeared in 1634; William Simpson's *The Second*

27

Book of Flowers, Fruits, Beasts, Birds and Flies, exactly drawn was published in 1650. These and various books on heraldry became sources of inspiration for new embroidery patterns, and their influence can be traced in contemporary samplers.

Of all the books used in this way, none, perhaps, was more popular than *La Clef des Champs*, published in 1586. Its author, Jacques Le Moyne de Morgues, tells us that he hoped it would be of service to all those who *'ayment et desirent d'apprendre choses bonnes et honnestes'*, namely painting, sculpture, goldwork, embroidery and tapestry. It contains about a hundred small, square woodcuts, treated decoratively and grouped two to the page. A few show birds and animals, but the majority are of fruit and flowers.

English random sampler. Silk and silver thread on linen. First half of 17th century.

Jacques Le Moyne de Morgues, born in Dieppe, was an artist and cartographer. In 1564 he participated in Laudonnière's expedition to relieve the French Huguenot colony that had been established in Florida. His instructions were 'to map the sea coast, and lay down position of towns, the depth and course of rivers and the harbours: and to represent also the dwellings of natives and whatever might seem worthy of observation.' His drawings were published, together with his account of the horrors of the treacherous Spanish attack upon Fort Carolina. Back home in France, Le Moyne de Morgues, who belonged to an eminent Calvinist family, narrowly escaped the St Bartholomew's Massacre. He took refuge in England, where he was befriended by Sir Walter Raleigh, who took him into his service.

Although books were becoming more widely available, they were still expensive. A sampler was still a good way of storing a repertoire of stitches and patterns. Worked on a long, narrow strip, often the entire width of a piece of linen, with selvedge top and bottom, they could be rolled up on a wooden or ivory roller and kept as an easy guide. New ideas or designs could be added at will. When Elizabeth Roberts set off for Boston, Massachusetts in 1672 with her second husband, Colonel Samuel Shrimpton, a rich American, she took with her two samplers she had worked around 1655, just before her first marriage. One shows elaborate running designs in colour

Oblong canvas panel traced with black outlines for embroidery. First half of 17th century.

of conventionalized flowers, 'boxers', intricate borders and a small amount of whitework. The second sampler is entirely devoted to drawn and cut work. Elizabeth Roberts was born in London in 1650, and the Massachusetts Historical Society has her portrait: a grave face, with large, dark eyes gazing pensively at the world. Her sombre but rich dress shows elaborate embroidery on the yoke and the sleeves. Her demure, elegant demeanour and long, white hands readily suggest long hours of patient sitting to create cobweb-like patterns on the linen of her cut-work sampler.

Despite the fact that it was done around 1655, Elizabeth Robert's sampler is typical of the style found at the beginning of the century: very long, narrow samplers, which acted as a personal record of stitches and designs. Gradually their purpose changed, as they became a means by which young girls were taught to sew. The meticulous rows of elaborate stitching were the equivalent

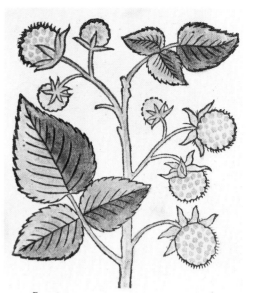

Above. Plate from *La Clef des Champs* by Jacques Le Moyne de Morgues (1586).

Left. Portrait of Elizabeth Roberts. She was born in England *c*1650 and, like Anne Gower, went to America. She married three times and died in Boston in 1713.

Mid 17th-century English sampler with examples of 'Boxers'.

of writing practice in an exercise book. 'Your schoole-mistress that can expound, and teaches to knit in chaldee, and make Hebrew samplers,' says a character in the play by Jasper Mayne, *The Citye Match*, written in 1639. This passage seems to indicate that by then samplers had become a part of the school curriculum for girls. Around that time, it also became common practice for samplers to include the date they were made and the name and age of the small girl who made them.

A. E. Tuer in his *History of the Horn Book* suggests that samplers were perhaps used to teach girls their letters. But it is far more likely that the need to mark the precious household linen with the initials or monogram of their owner explains the inclusion of alphabets in samplers.

> A Needle (though it be but small and slender)
> Yet it is both a maker and a mender:
> A graue Reformer of old rents decayd,
> Stops holes and seames, and desperate cuts displayed.
> And thus without the Needle we may see,
> We should without our Bibs and Biggins bee;
> No shirts or Smockes, our nakedness to hide,
> No garments gay, to make us magnifide:
> No shadowes, Shapparoones, Caules, Bands, Ruffs, Kuffs,
> No Kirchiefes, Quoyfes, Chin-clouts, or Marry-Muffes,
> No Cros-cloaths, Aprons, Hand-kerchiefes, or Falls,
> No Table-cloathes, for Parlours or for Halls.
> Nor any Garment man or woman weares.

The popularity of some of the earliest alphabets, which survived a good 250 years, is probably because the simple blocks forming the letters were so well suited to embroidery methods. But a more elaborate style of lettering, with curly flourishes in double-running stitch, also became very popular in the 17th century and survived into the 19th century—although only on Scottish and Dutch samplers.

Martha Edlin, who was born in 1660, finished a sampler at the age of eight. On a strip of linen in bright coloured silks she had worked three alphabets and 12 or more bands of ornament; she signed it 'Martha Edlin 1668'. The following year, she tackled a white work sampler: four bands of white thread embroidery and three of open lace-work, signed 'ME. 1669'. Such 17th-century strip patterns remained common until the late 18th century, when they turned into borders, framing much squarer pictorial embroideries—a style still used in the 20th century.

Two years later, Martha Edlin finished an embroidered cabinet. It contained pin-cushions, a needlecase, scent-bellows, and various small objects in needlework. The cabinet is embroidered with her name and the date, 1671. Her next task was to cover a flat oblong dressing box in bead work and silk embroidery on white satin. Figures of the seven virtues and their symbols are worked on the sides of the cabinet. A figure of Music is surrounded by groups representing the four elements. There are also animals— a lion, a unicorn, a camel or leopard, a stag and an elephant. A raised oval on the lid is decorated with an embroidered cockatrice. This box has her name and the date, 1673.

Not all little girls, however, delighted in the patient, time-consuming, gentle art of needlework. Lucy Hutchinson—born in 1619, the eldest daugh-

Late 17th-century band sampler. Coloured silk on linen worked in cross, eyelet and double-running stitches.

ter of Sir Allen Apsley, Lieutenant of the Tower of London—leaves us in no doubt about what she thought of the mountain of needlework she was expected to produce:

> When I was about seven years of age, I remember I had at one time eight tutors in several qualities, languages, music, dancing, writing, and needlework; but my genius was quite averse from all but my book, and that I was so eager of, that my mother thinking it prejudiced my health, would moderate me in it; yet this rather animated me than kept me back, and every moment I could steal from my play I would employ in any book I could find, when my own were locked up from me. After dinner and supper I still had an hour allowed me to play, and then I would steal into some hole or other to read. My father would have me learn Latin, and I was so apt that I outstripped my brothers who were at school, although my father's chaplain, that was my tutor, was a pitiful dull fellow. My brothers, who had a great deal of wit, had some emulation at the progress I made in my learning, which very well pleased my father; though my mother would have been contented if I had not so wholly addicted myself to that as to neglect my other qualities. As for music and dancing, I profited very little in them, and would never practise my lute or harpsichords but when my masters were with me; and as for my needle I absolutely hated it.

On the other hand, Hannah Smith, who was born before the end of the reign of Charles I, seemed to have enjoyed embroidery. In 1654, when she was almost twelve, she visited Oxford and spent her time there embroidering

Right. Examples of Martha Edlin's industry: coloured band sampler (1668), cut and drawn whitework sampler (1669). Her work box, made in 1671, is stumpwork on white satin.

Part of the sampler worked by ten-year-old
Frances Bridon in 1644.

the panels of her needlework cabinet. It must have meant a lot to her, as she left a written record of the event. This account, written in a neat and steady hand, is preserved, together with the box, at the Whitworth Art Gallery in Manchester:

the yere of Our Lord being 1657.

if ever I have any thoughts about the time when I went to Oxford, as it may be I may, when I have forgoten the time, to sartifi myself I may loock in this paper and find it; I went to Oxford in the yere of 1654 and my being thare near 2 years, for I went in 1654, and I stayed there 1655 and I cam away in 1656; and I was allmost 12 yers of age when I went, and I mad an end of my cabbinet at Oxford . . . and my cabbinet was mad up in the yere of 1656 at London. I have ritten this to sattisfi myself and thos that shall inquir about it. Hannah Smith.

The mastery of the needle was greatly helped by the technical progress of the age. During the reign of Mary Tudor, fine steel needles were introduced in England. They replaced iron needles, which had the great disadvantage of cutting through the thread. In view of this handicap, the beauty and skill displayed in early embroideries appear even more remarkable.

Portrait of a child, once thought to be Princess Elizabeth, daughter of James I, by Paul van Somer (*c*1576-1621). The apron has fine reticella edging and insertions.

Detail of a 17th-century whitework sampler with reticella patterns similar to those on the apron opposite.

Steel sewing needles came to Tudor England from the Far East, via the Middle East and Spain. The story goes that a dark-skinned man—some accounts claim he came from India, others that he was a Spanish Moor or a Negro—appeared at Mary's court with the first steel needle. His manufacturing secret was lost for a time after his death and by the end of the 16th century a needle was such a treasured possession that its loss could form the plot of a village comedy. In *Gammer Gurton's Needle*, written in 1575, the heroine bemoans the loss of:

My fair long straight needle that was mine only treasure
The first day of my sorrow is, and last of my pleasure

and turns the house upside down searching for it. Her neighbour is falsely accused of stealing it. A great brawl ensues and is settled only when the needle is discovered—pinned to the bottom of a pair of breeches Gammer Gurton had been mending.

Pins as well as needles were expensive and rare. According to tradition, pillow lace was introduced in England by Catherine of Aragon, who taught it to local women while staying at Ampthill, waiting to be divorced. Pillow lace was generally called 'bone' lace, because the country women who could not afford pins to prick out the patterns used fish bones or even long, stout thorns. Rich ladies used pins in great numbers to keep their elaborate and costly ruffs in place. From this practice comes the expression 'pin money'.

Since Elizabethan times, the town of Redditch, not far from Birmingham, has been the centre of the English needle trade. Redditch's official guide states: 'The origin of the needle industry in Redditch is obscure. It has been suggested that the art was understood by the monks of nearby Bordesley Abbey and that at the Dissolution they passed on their knowledge to local laymen.' By the 18th century, over 2,000 people of the district were employed in making needles by hand in their cottages. Gradually factories were established which carried out mechanically the preliminary cutting, straightening and pointing. But as late as 1882, Sophia F. Caufield and Blanche Saward, in their *Dictionary of Needlework*, reported that in the course of its manufacture every needle had to pass through 126 hands before it was ready for sale. All the most delicate operations, such as punching the eye, were done by hand.

Illustration from Diderot's *Encyclopédie* (Paris, 1751-80) showing some of the traditional skills involved in needle making: polishing, and sharpening.

PRACTICAL-17th CENTURY

DIAPER PATTERNS

The origins of most of the repeating patterns shown here remain obscure. It seems very likely, though, that they come from a common source, because they occur with remarkably little variation from sampler to sampler. The common stitches are tent stitch, rococo, Hungarian, Florentine stitches, French knots, and the characteristic plaited braid—in which a her-ringbone stitch is worked closely together with metallic thread, creating the effect of applied braid. The diapers illustrated are among those found most frequently. Although they may be worked in different colours and stitches, they remain almost constant in form. One of the most puzzling of the designs is no. 8—presumably a leaf. This peculiar drawing is copied faithfully on many samplers.

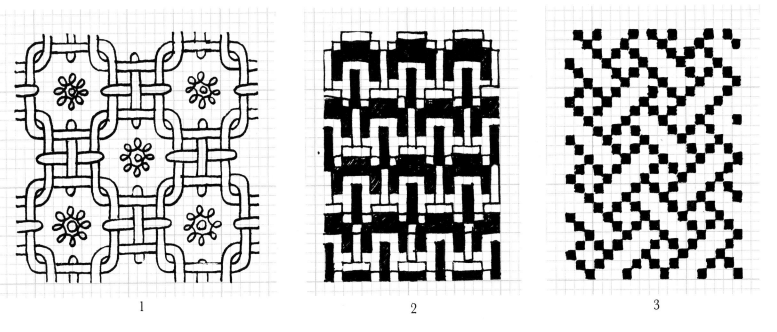

1

2

3

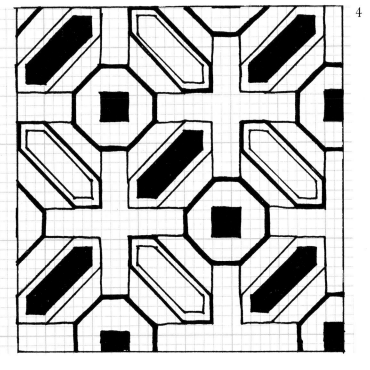

4

One pattern that is not always interpreted correctly is an arrangement of alternate obelisks and daisies. On one sampler it comes out as rows of fish; the plant leaves have been mistaken for tails.

Many such repeat designs were used on household textiles, clothes and small bags. Numerous examples survive.

1) Interlaced squares. Usually worked with a metallic plaited braid stitch, the centre loops being laid and couched down.

2) Overlapping design. Often shaded dark to light, worked in tent stitch.

3) Woven design. Worked in two or three colours in Algerian eye stitch, rococo stitch or in plaited braids.

4) Diaper squares. Usually worked in tent stitch, this pattern appears as a repeat of crosses, lozenges and other geometrical shapes, depending on which sections of the basic square patterns are most strongly coloured.

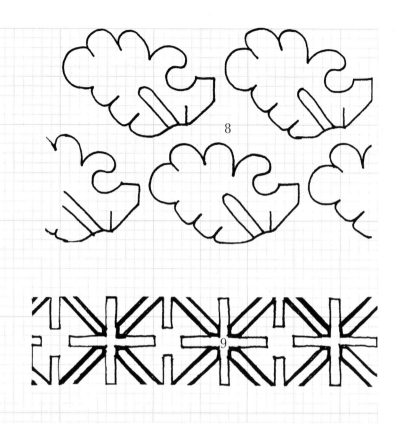

5) Linked circles. Worked in plaited metallic braid stitches with a tent stitch background, with couched or stem stitch and French knots.

6) Flower and circle chain. Made from a plaited braid with a French knot in the centre. The flower is filled with tent stitch; the circle contains a much used openwork background, made from hem stitch worked in rows and pulled tight to form a grid of holes.

7) Diaper pattern. This is usually arranged in three colours and is worked in Algerian eye stitch.

8) Repeat designs of leaves. These are generally alternately coloured pink, green and blue and are shaded from a dark outer line to a pale middle. Two stems are frequently made with plaited braid, as is the background where the braiding is done in horizontal rows. The leaves are in tent stitch.

9) Repeat diamonds. Worked in Hungarian stitch.

10) Box diaper pattern. The boxes and stems are often made with gold and silver plaited braid stitches; the rest is tent stitch. Leaves are shaded dark to light green, as are the acorn cups with yellow acorns. The background may be pale blue.

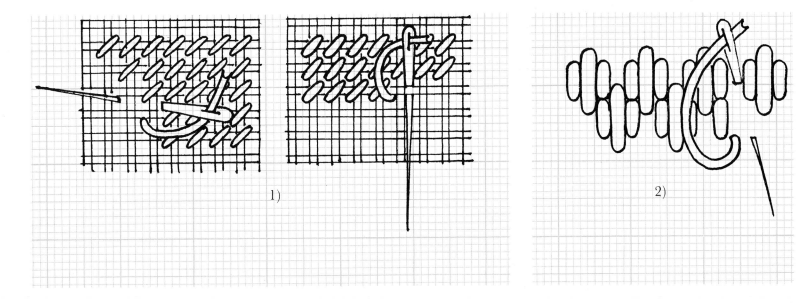

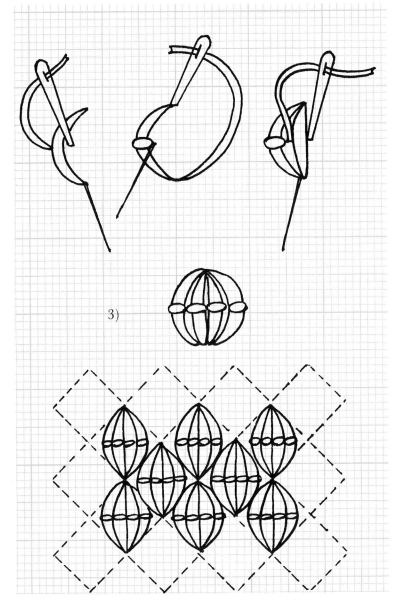

1) Tent stitch, also called *petit point*.
   a) Diagonal working fills large areas more evenly and with less tendency to pull one way.
   b) Tent stitch worked in horizontal rows.

2) Hungarian stitch. Spaced groups of three long and short satin stitches. Subsequent rows encroach.

3) Rococo stitch. Used as a solid filling stitch. It has the effect of little solid diamonds interspersed with small holes where the stitches meet. Stitches are worked encroaching on the previous row in a half-drop or diamond pattern. On samplers, this stitch was often worked extremely small and has the effect of a textured openwork.

4) Oriental stitch or Roumanian stitch, sometimes also called Roman stitch. Rococo stitch is a grouped version of Oriental stitch. When Oriental stitch is worked slanting it is known as Persian stitch.

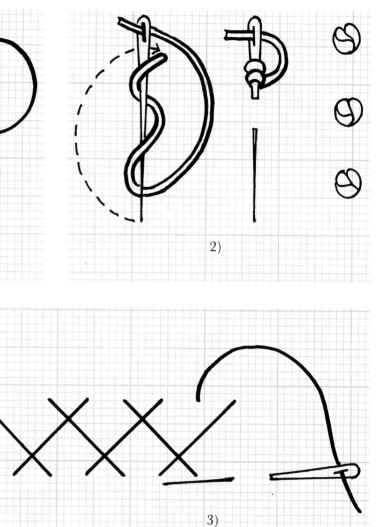

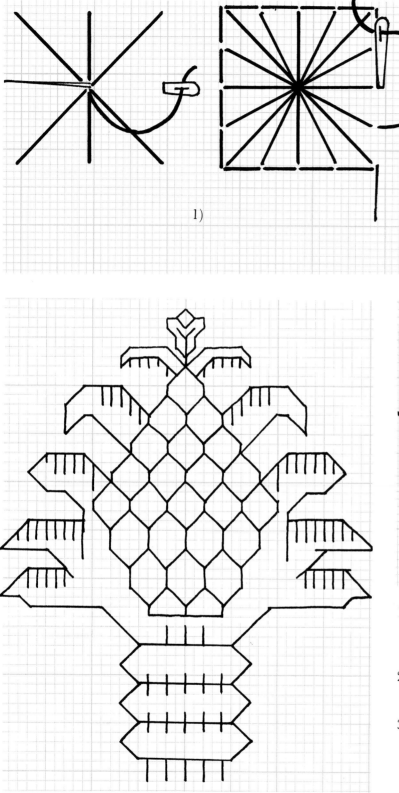

1) Algerian Eye and Eyelet stitch, which has twice as many stitches as an Algerian eye. It is finished off with a row of backstitches around the outer edge.

2) French knots. The thread is wrapped twice around the needle and put back into the same hole.

3) Herringbone stitch. Worked left to right. This stitch can be changed considerably by opening or closing the spacing and by varying the sizes of crosses and strokes.

Above. Pineapple motif in double running stitch. This is a sure sign of the influence exercised by illustrated books. The first actual pineapple did not reach England until several years after this symbol first appeared on samplers.

Opposite page. An example of 17th-century blackwork. Double running and filling stitches.

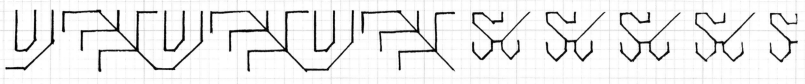

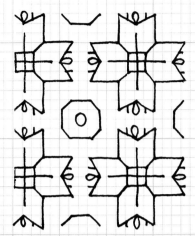
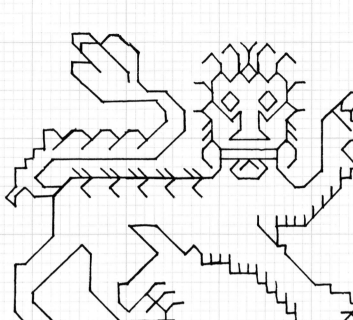

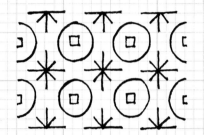
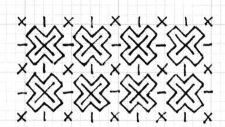

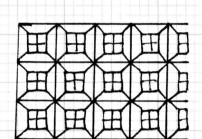
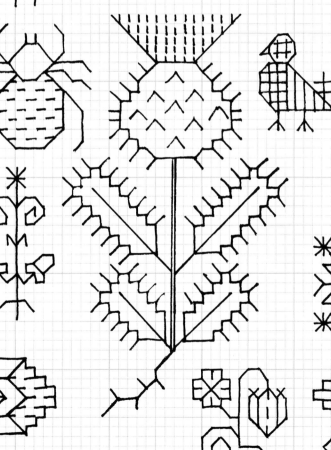
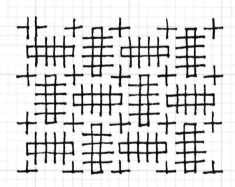

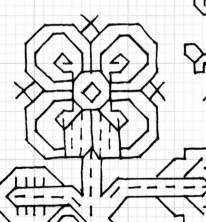

BOXERS

Of all the sampler motifs, the 'boxers and plant' pattern is the most curious and inexplicable. It appeared for the first time early in the 17th century as a row of little creatures, nude except for a fig leaf. They stand one foot in front of the other; with upraised arms they offer a trophy-like object to a huge, leafy plant. The repeats of the design are punctuated by a flower shape with arm-like branches.

This shape, on some samplers, appears to be a corruption of the human form. The origins of the boxer motif cannot be traced for certain. They do not seem to derive from either the early pattern books or the European folk tradition. Donald King points out that there does exist a traditional motif of lovers exchanging gifts under a tree. It has been suggested that a corrupted version of this motif was copied from a poor print and circulated, giving rise to the boxers.

Marcus Huish sees the boxers as Greek or Roman versions of Renaissance Cupids. Indeed, some boxers have curly wings on their shoulders and legs, although they might also represent Daphne pursued by Apollo.

The term boxer itself, however, is modern and derives from the figures' martial stance and upraised fists. The motif remained popular as a band design on samplers (usually done in double running stitch—blackwork) for well over a hundred years.

Towards the end of the 17th century, modesty or fashion prompted workers to clothe boxers in jerkins and drawers, stockings and shoes—even wigs. The basic outline remained the same, but it was filled in with satin or needlepoint stitches.

Occasional examples appeared on samplers as late as the 1750s. But by then they were often solitary spot motifs, with the plant shape often having disappeared.

It is evident that the exact nature of the boxer symbol was ambiguous even to the embroiderers: each interpreted the proffered gift or trophy according to her own inspiration. The most splendid examples consisted of tall vases. More often, however, a heart, a plant or a simple acorn was chosen.

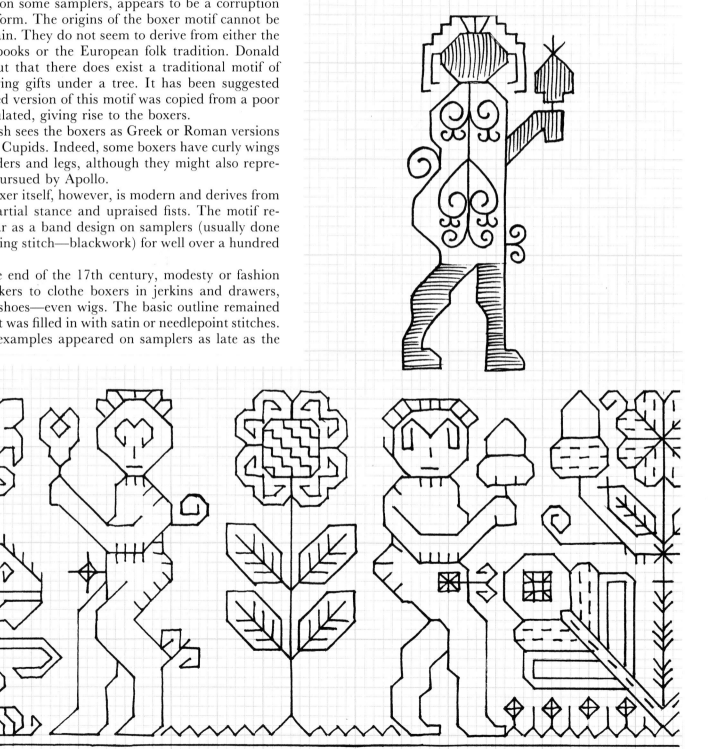

WHITEWORK

On 17th-century samplers, pulled and drawn thread work, reticella, lacis and satin stitch frequently appear together. Sometimes they form a separate whitework sampler.

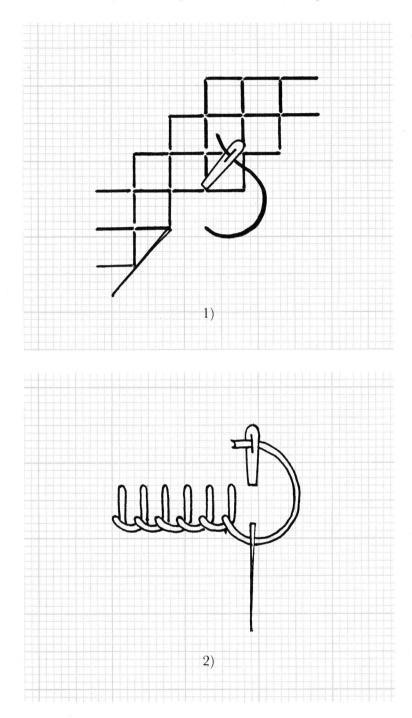

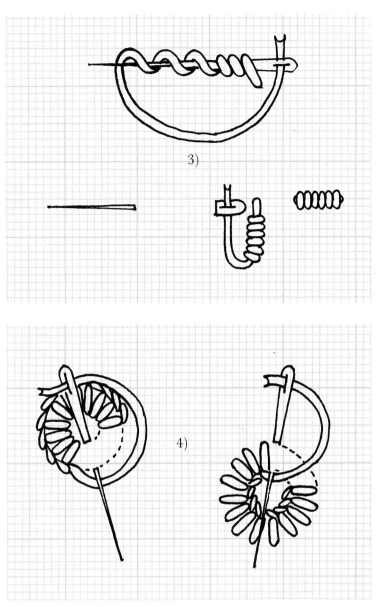

1) Single faggot or square stitch. Pulled tight on a loosely woven fabric, it will produce an open-work effect.

2) Buttonhole stitch. Stitches may be grouped in twos or threes, or the upright stitch can be variously angled or arranged in groups of long and short stitches.

3) Bullion bars or rolls are French knots with more twists. According to the length of bar required, twist the thread five, six or seven times around the needle and re-insert the needle a short distance away to form a neat ridged bar.

4) Buttonhole rings.
   a) Worked with the edge of the stitch on the outer contour.
   b) Worked out from the centre, which will have a more open effect that can be accentuated by enlarging the hole with a bodkin.

Opposite page, above. Boxer dressed in Renaissance curlicues. Worked in white double running stitch, face, arm and legs in dark red satin stitch. The figure holds a yellow acorn. (Sampler of Margaret Allen, Abbot Hall, Kendal, Cumbria.)

Opposite page, below. Mid 17th-century example of boxers.

TYPES OF WHITEWORK

Pulled thread work. Threads are not removed but are made into patterns by the use of embroidery stitches (varieties of cross and hemstitch or faggotting) drawn tight to produce holes and textures. This creates a contrast in the stiff geometric patterns. Straight rows of faggotting are used between patterns, chiefly in diaper diamond repeats; they are interspersed with Algerian eyelet holes and larger buttonhole rings with the edge of the stitch on the outside, radiating from a single hole which may be enlarged with a bodkin but is not cut. Pulled thread work is the negative version of the blackwork filling stitch.

Drawn thread work. Threads are cut and removed, either weft only, or warp and weft as in reticella. The remaining threads are overcast or needlewoven (Russian overcasting).

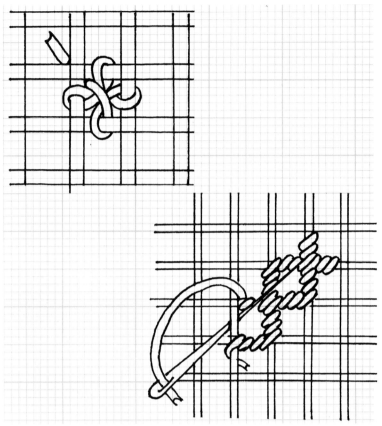

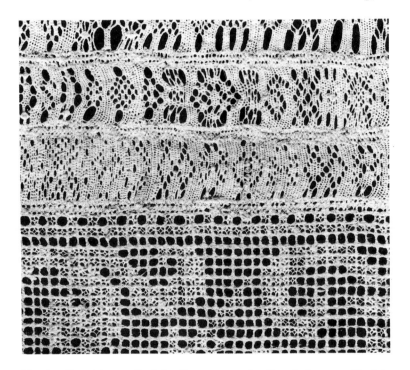

Above. Two versions of Russian overcasting.
  a) Used in drawn thread work where small scale grids or a lattice open-work background is required. In making grids for Reticella use needleweaving.
  b) Russian drawn filling. A filling for drawn thread squares, previously made with needleweaving or Russian overcasting.

Left. Detail of drawn thread and cut work.

Reticella. Also called Italian cutwork, Greek lace or Gothic point. A lace made by embroidery methods, it consists of arrangements of threads in the form of stars, crosses, checks and geometrical shapes, held together by needlewoven overcasting, buttonhole stitches and subsequent filling out with variations of buttonhole stitches produce textured solid areas. The more elaborate examples of reticella were pictorial.

On samplers, the grid framework is made by withdrawing warp and weft threads from an existing piece of fabric. The remaining bars are then needlewoven. Shapes are filled in with needle-made lace stitches, and loops and scallops are made by casting several threads across the space and buttonholing over them.

For use on collars, cuffs and clothing, reticella was formed by arranging and couching loose threads into the required grids and shapes on a coloured shift (waxed paper or fabric).

The lace was then worked and the coloured background was removed when the work was completed.

Vinciolo's 1587 pattern book contains many patterns for reticella work. In the most elaborate pictorial laceworks, details such as the folds in dresses, the centres and petals of flowers, were worked detached from the surface after the initial row of buttonholing. The result was a three-dimensional effect.

It is from knotting and cut work embroidery that bobbin lace derives. Cutwork was first made in nunneries around the 12th century, for use on robes and burial clothes. From the 15th to the 17th century, cutwork was taught by nuns but was widely made by aristocratic women. A small-size blunt tapestry needle is best for working both reticella filling and needlewoven bars as this prevents splitting the thread in the needle and the linen background.

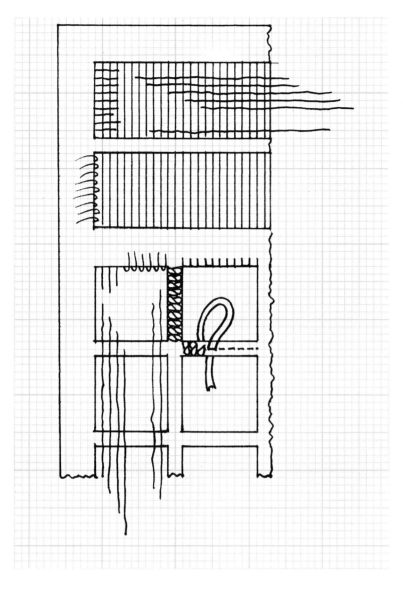

Preparing the fabric for Reticella.

Right.

1) Buttonhole bar. Buttonhole stitch over one or several threads to form a detached bar.

2) Adding a picot to a buttonhole bar. Used in Reticella work.

3) Needleweaving. Used to bind together two or more even numbers of threads in drawn work to produce solid bars and grids.

To work a piece of reticella

1) Choose a rather coarse, evenly woven linen or cotton, in which the threads will pull out easily. The thread used should be made of the same material as the fabric—for example, linen thread on linen—and should have about the same thickness. Do not use the waxed carpet variety of linen thread. Twisted embroidery cotton (*coton à broder*, Anchor) or fine crochet cotton is good. The thread should pass easily through a blunt, round-eyed needle.

2) Plan the grid by counting the threads, leaving even numbers to form the bars, which will be worked in pairs. It is often helpful to draw the grid lightly on the fabric with an HB pencil. Tack a piece of paper to the back of the fabric. This will keep the work square and firm while the threads are being removed and during the embroidery process. The pattern should leave a plain margin all round the fabric. Cut the threads at this margin and withdraw them. Buttonhole all around the raw edges. Start the work by needleweaving the grid bars. Begin the pattern at the narrowest part, taking a double thread from one corner to the other and working back along it with buttonhole stitch. Work each subsequent row into the loops of the previous one, increasing the number of stitches to form the shape. Where the pattern allows, anchor the end of each row to the grid bars.

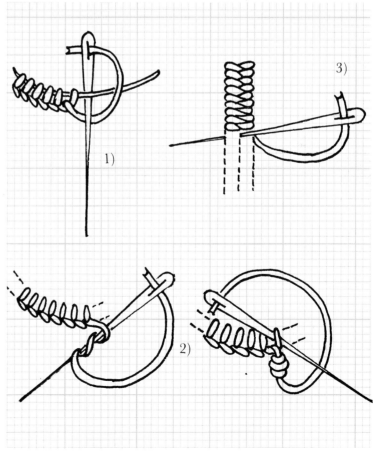

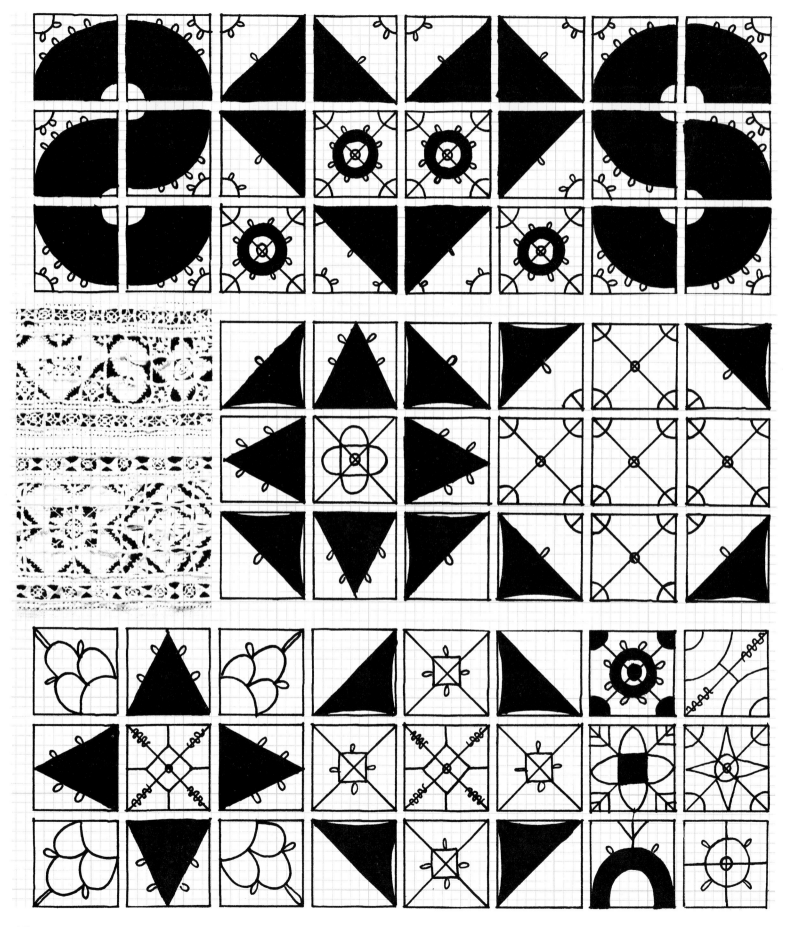

Lacis and reseau, or darned netting. Lacis is pattern darning on reseau, a handmade netting. On samplers this was done by withdrawing threads to form an open mesh, which was then strengthened with Russian overcasting. The pattern was darned in by filling it, square by square, with Russian drawn filling stitch, a simple stitch which loops around the mesh.

Half of Vinciolo's pattern book and many later books, contain diagrams for this kind of work. Besides the usual arcaded carnation, acorn and tulip designs one of the commonest is that of a hare being chased by a hound.

Darned netting had already been worked in the Middle Ages. The earliest English reference is a piece dated 1295 in St Paul's Cathedral. During the 19th century there was a revival, using machine-made net; coarser work was produced under the names of hairpin work and filet crochet.

FLATSTITCH OR SATIN STITCH
This embroidery was usually worked with lightly twisted white linen thread on a white or buff linen background. It appears at the bottom of the long polychrome band samplers, or as part of a separate whitework sampler alongside reticella cutwork and darned netting. Having little or no contrast, it relies for effect on a variety of raised surface treatments to give an embossed, tactile quality as well as on the play of light which changes with the angle of the stitches.

Some of the designs are intricate, all-over repeat patterns in stepped diapers. Others are the same as the coloured band designs, or simple geometric blocks. They are worked by counting threads, which are barely visible on fine linen. However, these designs work very well enlarged and with a correspondingly thicker thread such as a soft embroidery cotton or linen thread on hessian or crash. The blocks of satin stitches are generally worked in an upright or horizontal direction rather than in the radiating lines of 18th-century pictorial embroidery. The flat, even solids are contrasted with cut buttonhole slots and wheels, buttonhole and bullion stitch bars and loops, eyelets and double running stitches. The square stitch diagonals are sometimes drawn tight, to produce openwork holes. The loops and bars should be made slightly longer than the space they are meant to fill, so that they stand up slightly.

Letters and figures were also worked solid in flat stitch. The letter forms were the same as those later used for cross stitch: angular letters worked in stepped blocks with divided serifs (see endpapers for patterns).

Opposite page. Reticella cut work pattern. The grids represent needlewoven bars while the black sections are solid areas, worked in buttonhole stitch with picot edging. The rest of the design is filled with connecting bars, worked in button-hole over a cast thread. The photograph of a portion of a sampler shows typical Reticella patterns.

Above. Mid 17th-century English whitework sampler in flat stitch.

Below.
Left. Flat stitch, an encroaching satin stitch.
Right. Florentine stitch.

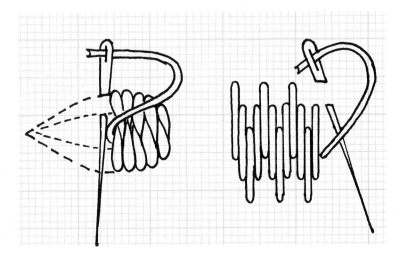

48

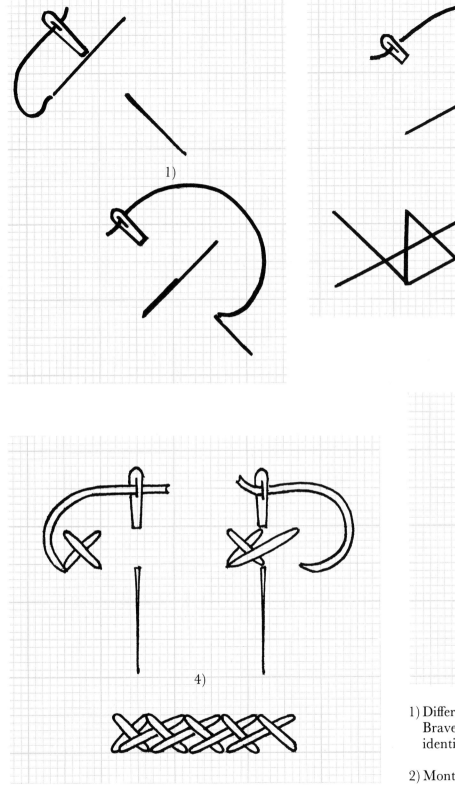

1) Different kinds of cross stitch were used in the 17th century. Brave bred stitch or double sided cross stitch produces an identical effect on both sides of the fabric.

2) Montenegrin cross stitch. Worked in three stages.

3) Long armed or long legged cross stitch. Start a row with an ordinary cross stitch. The long arm should be twice the length of the short stitch.

4) Crosslet, more frequently called rice stitch.

Opposite page. Flat stitch patterns.

1,2) Double running or square stitch diagonals with buttonholed loops and bars.

3) Satin stitch and Algerian eyelets.

4,5) Flat or satin stitch.

49

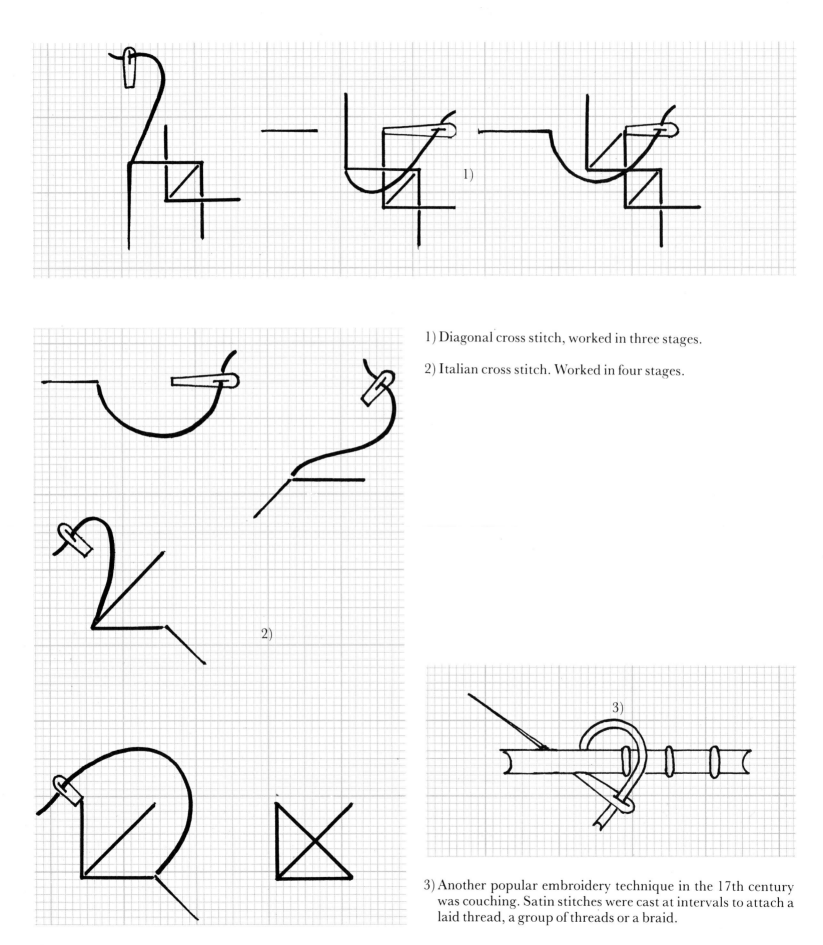

1) Diagonal cross stitch, worked in three stages.

2) Italian cross stitch. Worked in four stages.

3) Another popular embroidery technique in the 17th century was couching. Satin stitches were cast at intervals to attach a laid thread, a group of threads or a braid.

THE EIGHTEENTH CENTURY

But here the needle plies its busy task
The pattern grows, the well-depict'd flower
Unfold its bosom, buds and leaves and sprigs,
And curling tendrils, gracefully disposed,
Follow the nimble fingers of the fair;
A wreath that cannot fade, of flowers that blow
With most success when all besides decay.

William Cowper,
The Task, (written in 1784 and addressed to Mrs Delany)

In the early 18th century, England was a country of hamlets and villages. The few sizeable towns were situated along the coast. A few urban centres were beginning to evolve in Lancashire, the West Riding of Yorkshire and the West Midlands, but on the whole the population remained rural and was still concentrated in the south.

It is difficult to estimate the population of the time, but it seems likely to have been about 5,500,000 by 1714. Between 1714 and 1742, there was only a very small increase in population, but important changes in its distribution took place. East Anglia showed a decline. The West Country, the South and the East Midlands remained static; so did the East Riding and all of the North except for Tyneside, the West Riding, South Lancashire and the West Midlands, which showed a large increase. Surrey and Middlesex developed with London, which maintained the rapid expansion shown in the late 17th century. London's population was thought to exceed half a million; Bristol may have had 50,000. Manchester, Liverpool, Sheffield, Leeds, Halifax, Birmingham, and Coventry all ceased to be the sprawling villages of fifty years earlier. Although small by modern standards—they all had less than 50,000 inhabitants—they nevertheless absorbed an endless flow of people, and their population was only maintained by continuous immigration from the countryside and from Ireland.

The reasons for these trends are not difficult to find. In the early 18th century, only about one child in four born in London survived. Infant mortality was probably even higher in the mushrooming towns of the North. Due to overcrowding and lack of sanitation, disease was rampant and unchecked: smallpox, typhus, typhoid and dysentery were common causes of death. Dr Johnson's *London* and accounts by foreign and English travellers give us an idea of the squalor and harsh living which reigned in the metropolis. London was at the time a place of strong contrasts: luxury and elegance side by side with poverty and ugliness.

Urban society was dominated by the merchant princes. Their ideal was to purchase great estates, thereby acquiring the prestige carried by land

ownership. Their sons and daughters would then be able to marry into the aristocracy or acquire a title in their own right. This life-style differed little from that of the nobility: they built just as grandly and spent fabulous amounts on furniture, food and servants. Their financial ties with the government were strong and they were supporters of Walpole, upholding the Hanoverian dynasty, believing in keeping things as they were.

The great majority of 18th-century merchants, however, were prosperous shopkeepers whose habits of life were still deeply rooted in the 17th century. They remained attached to puritan ideals and lived simple, industrious and thrifty lives.

Midway between the rich and the poor were the craftsmen and artisans, journeymen and apprentices of the great livery companies of London. They worked about fourteen hours a day for a modest wage which, combined with those of their wives and children, enabled them to live decently so long as trade was good. But they remained at the mercy of any sudden fall in the market or of changes in industrial organization—the decline of the old guilds, the spread of a free labour market and particularly the introduction of labour-saving machinery. Nevertheless, they were well off compared with the greater mass of London's population—labourers, dependent on casual employment, whose lot in life could change overnight from modest affluence to abject poverty. Hogarth's prints of London life recall the lean faces and shrunken bodies of such poor people. Not infrequently, they expressed their despair in riots. Their plight may have been the concern of benevolent men such as Coram and Oglethorpe; to politicians, it was a nightmare.

Despite the harshness of life in 18th-century London, it was also a place full of opportunities for men of determination: with wealth and property came standing in society. At least in the early part of the century, it was fairly easy to pass from one social class to another—a fact that was observed with great wonder by Voltaire and other contemporaries.

In the countryside, however, life had remained more or less static, controlled firmly by tradition and custom. The great majority of small farmers tilled the soil in the manner their forebears had for centuries. Only large landowners had the financial backing required to experiment with new ideas and techniques. The demand for wool and corn made farming and, therefore, the acquisition of ever larger estates a very profitable investment. In every country a few aristocratic families possessed similar wealth. This set them apart from the small landowners, the squires. This distinction was further emphasized by the way of life these people had created for themselves. Ostentatious wealth was no offence in their eyes: Castle Howard, Wentworth Woodhouse, Houghton were the admiration and the envy of all. These great houses were overflowing with treasures: Italian fire-places, French furniture and tapestries. Asia had also been ransacked: textiles and precious objects from India, lacquer and porcelain from China. The countryside around these houses was remodelled to form a suitable setting. Trees and plants which have now become very common in gardens and the countryside were then coveted novelties: the weeping willow, for instance, the acacia and the fuchsia were introduced in the early part of the 18th century. The character of the gardens was changing—the formal lines, the symmetrically clipped trees were losing favour. Landscape gardeners were fascinated by the meandering lines of Chinese gardens, with their rocks and artificial hills, their succession of carefully planned scenes that nevertheless gave an illusion of

natural landscape. Joseph Addison, the editor of *The Spectator*, expressed this rejection of Western tradition when he wrote: 'Our British Gardeners instead of humouring Nature, love to deviate from it as much as possible. Our Trees rise in Cones, Globes, and Pyramids. We see the Marks of the Scissors upon every Plant and Bush. I do not know whether I am singular in my Opinion but for my own part, I would rather look upon a Tree in all its Luxuriancy and Diffusion of Boughs and Branches, than when it is thus cut and trimmed into a Mathematical Figure; and cannot but fancy that an Orchard in Flower looks infinitely more delightful than all the little Labyrinths of the most finished Parterre.'

This yearning for a more naturalistic approach was also reflected in embroidery which was strongly influenced by Indian and Chinese motifs. The painted flower of Indian chintzes seemed a revelation to Western eyes, and their designs were adopted by embroiderers and appeared alongside the fashionable Chinoiserie. Silk-embroidered pagodas and exotic gardens adorned the dresses of fashionable ladies. A book entitled *The Embassy to the Grand Tartar* by John Nieuhof, translated into English in 1669, had offered a glimpse of the beautiful gardens that surrounded the Imperial Palace in Peking. Its illustrations of bridges and pagodas inspired many English gardeners to build similar decorative follies. The pagoda and the Chinoiserie pavilion in the Royal Botanical Gardens at Kew, near London, are striking reminders of this craze.

The affinity between contemporary embroidered motifs and fashionable

Above left. Engraving by Jean Pillement for Robert Sayer's *The Ladies Amusement* (1760) demonstrating the craze for 'Chinoiserie' or 'Cathay' which spread through England in the 18th century.

Above right. 'Chinoiserie' English printed cotton, 1760.

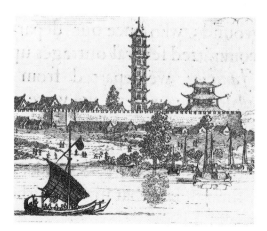

Rest in peace brian :(

Above left. Late 17th-century painted cotton from South India.

Above centre. English floral chintz. Second half of the 18th century.

Above right. Detail from an 18th-century man's waistcoat. Embroidered in coloured silks laid with cotton net and edged with chenille.

Below left. September flowers from Robert Furbers *The Flower Garden Display'd* (1732) '...very useful not only for the curious in gardening, but the prints likewise for Painters, Carvers, Japanners etc. also for the Ladies as patterns for working, and painting in watercolours, or furniture for the closet.'

Below right. Similar flowers copied on a silk embroidered picture by Edith Hucheson at Mrs Rosco's Boarding School, Bristol, 1769. This was a precursor of 19th-century fancy work and a very different task from the more workaday ones set for charity girls a century later (see page 83).

Opposite. 'Kiangsi' from Jan Nieuhof's *An Embassy from the East India Company of the United Provinces* (the Dutch East India Company), *to the Grand Tartar Cham Emperour [sic] of China* (1699).

garden design was no coincidence. The same people often produced designs for both. Crewel work was one of the most popular needlework types in 18th-century England. Dresses, men's waistcoats, curtains, hangings and bed covers were ablaze with it. Lady Llanover described an extravagant petticoat belonging to Mrs Delany, the 18th-century diarist, embroideress and garden designer: it was 'covered with sprays of natural flowers, in different positions, including the bugloss, auriculas, honeysuckle, wild roses, lilies of the valley, yellow and white jessamine, interspersed with small single flowers. The border at the bottom being entirely composed of large flowers,

SEPTEMBER

Edith Hutcheson. Dec.r 1769. don

in the manner in which they grow.' Whitework, so popular in the previous century, was still fashionable, but the patterns used were different. Here again, the influence of Chinoiserie was evident: strangely shaped rocks adorned with pagodas and exotic trees were exquisitely worked on fine muslins and used on articles such as aprons and fichus.

Using a technique derived from Indian embroidery, beautiful silk bed covers and hangings were also produced. The work was done entirely in chain stitch. Later in the century, this type of work was made on a small circular frame, not with a needle but with a hook which drew a loop of thread to the surface from below the cloth. By reinserting the hook and repeating the operation, stitches were formed very quickly. The frame and the hook were probably developed in France—hence the name *tambour*, drum, by which this type of work came to be known.

Another 18th-century English craze was knotting, which was probably introduced from Holland in the late 17th century. For this type of work a shuttle was used, consisting of two oval blades made of bone, ivory, mother of pearl or tortoise-shell, pointed at both ends and joined in the middle. The size of the shuttle depended on the thickness of the thread or cord. After filling the shuttle, the worker held it in her right hand and passed it through the loop of the thread held by the left hand. This produced knots at regular intervals. The knotted thread or cord was then couched down with small stitches, following a pattern drawn on the cloth. Knotted work was used a great deal for chair covers and hangings.

For all the beautiful embroidery produced during the 18th century, contemporary samplers did not by any means show the wealth of stitches that other types of work displayed. The function of the sampler had changed. Instead of being used as a record of stitches by adult ladies or young girls, 18th-century samplers were mostly the work of small schoolgirls, often five or six years old. Being schoolroom products, the samplers consisted largely of alphabets and numerals.

The shape of samplers was also slowly beginning to change. Although long, narrow samplers were still made in the 1730s, the sampler became increasingly square—a shape suitable for framing and mounting on the wall. The vogue for Indian printed cottons had also left its mark. Colours became brighter, and there was a tendency towards more realistic floral patterns in flowing lines rather than the stiffer, angular motifs found on earlier samplers. In effect, the picture sampler familiar to us today had arrived. Pots of flowers, fruit trees, birds, members of the family, shepherdesses, Adam and Eve, rabbits, pet dogs: all were arranged symmetrically around a verse.

As the century advanced, religious and moral verses came more and more into fashion. This trend was undoubtedly linked with the advent of Methodism: it followed closely on the publication of Isaac Watt's *Divine and Moral Songs for Children* (1720), and the hymns of Wesley (1736) and Dr. Doddridge (1738). The Lord's Prayer, the Ten Commandments and other Biblical texts appeared framed as tablets. The passion for lettering and ardent Protestantism reached a joint climax in samplers that reproduced entire chapters from the Bible.

Marcus Huish mentions samplers made in an Orphan's School near Calcutta. Six of the pupils were given the task of working between them the longest chapter in the Bible, the 119th Psalm. They performed the task

Susannah Cochran's sampler, made in 1792, expresses characteristic sentiments.

Opposite. Elizabeth Knowles's Perpetual Almanack made at Walton School in 1787 provides an idea for a sampler which can still be worked today.

Perpetual Almanack

Years

A	G	F	E	D	C	B
	1787		88	89	90	91
	92	93	94	95		96
97	98	99	1800	1	2	3
		4	5	6	7	8
9	10	11		12	13	14
15		16	17	18	19	
20	21	22	23		24	25
26	27		28	29	30	31
	32	33	34	35		36
37	38	39		40	41	42
43		44	45	46	47	

Months (centre table)

January / October
May
August
February / March / November
June
September / December
April / July

Sundays

1	2	3	4	5	6	7
8	9	10	11	12	13	14
15	16	17	18	19	20	21
22	23	24	25	26	27	28
29	30	31				
A	B	C	D	E	F	G
B	C	D	E	F	G	A
C	D	E	F	G	A	B
D	E	F	G	A	B	C
E	F	G	A	B	C	D
F	G	A	B	C	D	E
G	A	B	C	D	E	F

Explanation.

Under the Word Years find the Year, above which is the Dominical Letter for that Year, then against the Month in the other Table find the same Letter over which are placed the Days of the Month for every Sunday of that Month.

Elizabeth Knowles fecit

Walton School 1787

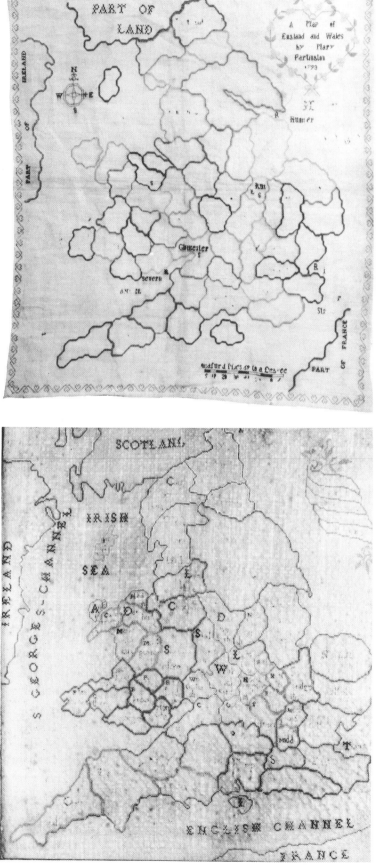

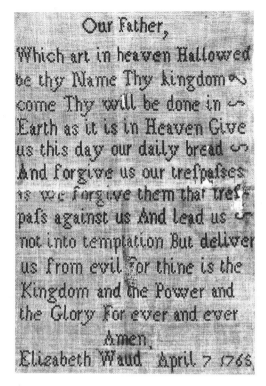

Above. The Lord's Prayer worked by Elizabeth Waud in black silk on linen.

Opposite, top left. Ann Brasher's sampler, 1789.

Opposite, top right. Unfinished map sampler of England and Wales, 1793. Silk on linen. Worked in cross and blanket stitches.

Opposite, below left. A 19th-century example of the map games which were often used as a basis for drawing a map sampler. This is a dissected map of England on wood made as a jigsaw puzzle.

Opposite, below right. A typical map sampler of the British Isles.

under the direction of Mistress Parke............who obviously believed in preserving the principles of Christian............in pagan Bengal. The whole job was completed between the 1........February and the 23rd of June in 1797. The top of each sampler showed a different view of the school.

If a sampler of the time did not include a religious verse, it was likely to carry one about children's duties to their parents, or it might warn the child against the dangers of fickle love, in the manner of a sampler made by Elizabeth Bock in 1764:

Oh Might God that knows how inclinations lead
Keep mine from straying lest my Heart should bleed.

Grant that I honour and succour my parents dear
Lest I should offend him who can be most severe.

I implore oer me you'd have a watchful eye
That I may share with you those blessings on high.

And if I should by a young youth be Tempted
Grant I his schemes defy and all He has invented.

Even on more pictorial samplers, the range of stitches was rather limited, and fashionable embroidery techniques did not appear. But though the repertoire of stitches was relatively small, it was nevertheless executed with great proficiency.

Around 1770, map samplers became popular, reflecting an increase in the public interest in geography and in journals of foreign travel. The England of villages and small market towns had been catapulted into the modern age by the trauma of the industrial revolution. At the beginning of the century, few people ventured far afield. Roads were few and responsibility for their repair was left to the inhabitants of the parish through which they passed—which meant that roads were never repaired until their state became desperate. It was said that men and horses drowned in the pot-holes of the Great North Road. Highwaymen lay in wait for weary travellers and were the despair of merchants whose goods they regularly plundered. But between 1750 and 1770, considerable economic and social changes took place and London became a metropolis in the modern sense. Improved communications with the rest of the country became an absolute necessity. By the 1770s, road engineering had greatly improved. Mail coaches for the rapid transport of letters and passengers were introduced in 1784. In 1754, it had taken four and a half days to travel from London to Manchester; by 1788, the journey took only 28 hours.

Improved communications also meant that news travelled faster. London news was printed in Liverpool within two days. People's horizons were widening. Education, even for girls, received more prominence. It is quite possible, in fact, that the making of map samplers was seen as an easy way to teach small children geography and needlework at the same time.

The copper plates of Saxton's *Atlas*, originally published in 1579, were reprinted. The interest in geography was soon turned into a new source of inspiration for embroiderers, thanks to John and Thomas Jeffreys, and above all to the enterprising John Spilsbury. He was the first printer to hit upon the idea of printing the outlines of these maps straight on white silk or satin. Some such samplers were then worked in black thread, probably to resemble more closely the original engraving, while others were embroidered in various hues to distinguish the countries.

Other maps were obviously drawn by hand, and this led to some surprising results. In one map, the little embroiderer obviously thought that England and France had a common boundary. On others, place names were arranged haphazardly: in one, for example, London appears somewhere north of Sheffield. Although maps of England were most common, many children produced maps of their own counties. Maps of the Old World or the New World, of Africa and of individual European countries were also made.

Two other types of 18th-century samplers were darning samplers and Hollie point samplers. The former displayed a variety of darning stitches, worked on the cloth by the counted thread method. These darns were also often worked over a cut-out hole or an L-shaped tear, the exercises serving as a useful training for the future housewife, who would have to repair her own precious stock of damask household linen.

Hollie point samplers were reminiscent of the whitework samplers from previous centuries. Probably worked by adult needlewomen, Hollie point samplers differed from other types in that they illustrated motifs and techniques that would have been used on articles of dress—particularly children's clothes.

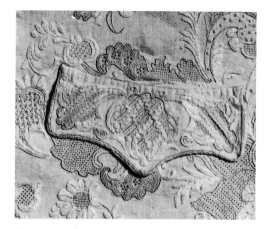

Drawn thread work on an early 18th-century waistcoat. Cotton and linen thread.

Five pieces patched together to form a sampler. Worked in coloured silks on loosely woven canvas, 1785.

60

Sarah Lowell, born 10th April 1738, made this sampler in Boston, Massachusetts in 1750. Silk on linen. Worked in cross, satin and tent stitches, $17\frac{3}{4} \times 12\frac{1}{2}$in.

If the 17th century is rightly regarded as the golden age of the sampler in England, the 18th century certainly saw the coming of age of the American sampler. Few samplers made on American soil during the 17th century have survived. We know of Loara Standish's work, which appears to be the earliest truly American sampler. (Anne Gower's sampler, already described, had been worked in England.) Loara's sampler was identical in style to contemporary English-made examples. It is a band sampler without an outer border, with a very intricate design, finely worked on a tabby weave linen (known as plain weave in Britain) in two weights of silk, in shades of cream, green, yellow, brown, buff and blue. The sampler includes Loara's name and a verse:

> Laora [sic] Standish is my name
> Lorde Guide My Hart That
> I May Doe they Will also Fill

> My hands With Such con-
> Venient Skil as May
> Conduce to Vertue Void of
> Shame and I will give
> Glory Lord to they name

The sampler is undated but we know that it was worked before 1655. In that year, Loara's father, Captain Miles Standish of the Plymouth Colony, mentioned that she predeceased him. We know that her year of birth was 1623, and it is reasonable to assume that she made her sampler before reaching the age of twenty—in other words, around 1643. The sampler now adorns the Pilgrim Hall at Plymouth.

Another early American sampler is that of Mary Hollingsworth of Salem. Born in 1650, she must have made her sampler around 1665, some ten years before her marriage to a local merchant, Phillip English. It was also worked on a fine tabby linen, in pink, blue and green silks. There is a large variety of stitches forming pretty borders with pansies, strawberries, roses, acorns and honeysuckle. The sampler was obviously valued by her family: one of her descendants painstakingly described it in his will and indicated that the patterns were intended for shawl borders.

These two samplers and other 17th-century specimens such as Sarah Lord's, made in 1668, had all been created in New England. Pennsylvania, which contributed so many samplers in the second half of the 18th century and in the 19th century, does not have any recorded earlier specimen.

Sarah Lord's sampler is of particular interest because it begins to show the characteristics of American samplers. It is shorter and broader than its predecessors. With the advent of the 18th century, New England samplers became nearly square, and developed a border—often on three sides only, while the focal point of the sampler became the far more pictorial lower portion. A verse was almost always included in the design.

Life became more settled in 18th-century America. As people became less worried about bare subsistence, they could aspire to a more refined way of living. Dame schools sprang up everywhere. These little schools taught very young children, and, just as in England, sampler-making was part of their programme. Their samplers were very simple, containing only alphabets and numerals, and probably served the dual purpose of teaching the necessary skill of marking fine household linen—which was often still spun and woven at home—and helping the children to learn their letters and numbers. For girls from ordinary homes, this instruction probably constituted their entire schooling. Boys' education was regarded as important very early on, but until the Revolution a girl was considered educated once she could read the New England Primer.

Opposite: Patty Coggeshall, born in 1780, came from Bristol, Rhode Island. Her sampler, worked c1795, is in vari-coloured silks on canvas. Embroidered in satin, petit-point and rococo stitches.

ABCDEFGHIJKLMNOPQRST
VUWXYZ&

If I Am Right Oh Teach My Heart
Still In The Right To Stay
If I Am Wrong Thy Grace Impart
To Find The Better Way

'Mary Batchelder was born June the 13 1757 wrought this sampler 1773.' A very carefully designed and worked sampler, in silk on linen. The stitches include eyelet, satin, cross, stem, half-cross, chain, long and short, rococo variations, fishbone, Roumanian and surface satin as well as French knots. $16\frac{1}{4} \times 11$in.

Above left. This lovely sampler was made by Abigail Mears in 1772. Scenes of dogs chasing a stag were embroidered on both European and American samplers throughout the 17th and 18th centuries. This hunting scene contains satin, surface satin, stem and split stitches. The border is worked in cross and satin stitches with a cross stitch alphabet above the verse and one in eyelet stitch below. Silk and cotton on cotton. 19 × 15¼in.

Above right. Polly Turner's sampler was made in the renowned school run by Mary (Polly) Balch in 1786. The building in the centre is the President's house at Brown University. The embroidery was done through newspaper (dated May 19, 1786), and the inked outline is still visible under the outside trails of the floral border. Silk and metallic embroidery on linen, 14½ × 11in.

Parents who could afford it would send their daughters to finishing schools, where they would be taught the accomplishments of proper young ladies. The press displayed many advertisements like the following, which comes from the *Boston News-Letter*, dated 19th April 1714:

At the House of Mr James Ivers, formerly call'd Bowling Green House, in Cambridge Street, Boston, is now set up a Boarding School where there will be carefully taught Flourishing, Embroidery, and all sorts of Needlework; also Filigree, Painting upon Glass, Writing, Arithmetic and singing Psalm Tunes.

The samplers worked by young ladies at such establishments were far more elaborate affairs, with some elements of individuality.

Mary Daintery made a sampler in 1721. Rectangular, with a delicate floral border, it is regarded as the first sampler with a border all round it. The figure of Christ appears in the middle of the top portion of the sampler. The entire remaining space is given to a long passage of Publius Lentulus's Letter to the Senate of Rome. It is followed by the inscription, 'Mary Daintery her work done in the year of our Lord AD 1721', and the date of her birth, 1713. It seems incredible that a child of eight would have had the patience to sit the many hours required to embroider such a long text, and such concern with religious things at such an early age also appears surprising. Her work is of particular interest because it is the first sampler with a distinctively American feel about it. This is another New England sampler, having been made at New Haven, Connecticut.

Three years later, in 1724, the first dated Pennsylvania sampler was made by Susanna Painter, of Philadelphia, who was seven years old. Samplers made three years later by Mary Morris and Ann Marsh are still band samplers with borders reminiscent of the 17th century. The style is understandable, since Ann Marsh was an English girl and in England the band sampler survived well into the 18th century.

The middle of the 18th century presents a difficulty: that of drawing a line between embroidered pictures and the increasingly pictorial trend in

'Elizabeth Couch was born the 29 of October, 1727 on the day of the great earthquake. Finished 1738.' Silk on linen. Worked in crewel stitch. $16\frac{1}{4} \times 13$in.

samplers. In their book on American samplers, Ethel Stanwood Bolton and Eva Johnston Coe made an admittedly somewhat arbitrary ruling by declaring that all needlework which was signed and dated by its author would be considered a sampler. Mary or Martha Bulyn's sampler, made in 1730, is a case in point. The cloth, embroidered all over like a picture, shows a shepherdess standing under a tree and watching her flock. The lack of proportion in the design is an added charm: a bird nearly the size of a sheep sits on the tree, while an enormous flower, almost half of the tree's height rises from the ground on the left. Pictorial as it is, the work is nevertheless signed and dated, and it therefore ranks as a sampler.

One of the most beautiful New England samplers was made in 1743 by Mary Fleet of Boston. It is square, with a lovely floral border, the ground of which is covered with Florentine stitch. The centre of the sampler is filled with crossbands, all very different in character. The stitches include cross-stitch outline, satin, long and short, and Florentine stitch. The silks in the border shimmer like enamel.

Around 1750, the sampler had become a much freer and more original form of work than it had been at the beginning of the century. While making their samplers, girls included many more elements from the world around them: landscapes, animals, and real people wearing contemporary fashions rather than allegorical figures like Adam and Eve. The little embroideresses showed great inventiveness. Clothes on figures were often appliquéd on the canvas. The lady shown on Elizabeth Pecker's sampler, made in 1750 sported an appliquéd skirt, as well as a beautiful head of hair made from a lock of real reddish-grey hair. A variety of materials had begun to be used to make the stitchery more realistic and to underline its beauty: beads and sequins, metallic threads, painted paper and even mica. Perhaps it is the fact that American samplers reflected so much of the personality of each individual little girl or her teacher that gives them so much charm.

This is particularly noticeable in school samplers, for which many schools evolved a definite style. In the 1750s, a school near Boston used the popular image of Adam and Eve, and this motif recurs again and again, interpreted in different ways. Of course, not all designs produced in schools showed great originality. Some seemed, in fact, more like a punishment than an exercise in needlework. Mary Ellis, of Milton, Massachusetts, was required to divide the centre of her sampler into a hundred diamond-shaped spaces. A multiplication table was embroidered on the diamond.

In the 1760s, the pious verse became an integral part of the sampler. These verses worked by children on their samplers hold a peculiar fascination. Why did they choose these moral axioms, the tag ends of hymns and verses? The puritan severity of these texts seems strangely inappropriate today and far beyond the understanding of an average child. The Lord's Prayer, the Ten Commandments and quotations from Isaac Watt's *Divine and Moral Songs*, appear on many samplers. This preoccupation with Sin and Death among young children is disconcerting. It is puzzling why a ten-year-old girl should select:

> Who is this trembling Sinner, who
> That owns Eternal Dark his due
> That mourns his sins, his guilt, his thrall
> And does on God for Mercy call?

68

Sarah Afflick, from Philadelphia, made this sampler when she was only seven. The original drawing is still visible on the fabric underneath the embroidery. Silk on cotton. Worked in stem, chain, satin, buttonhole wheel, cross, Roumanian, fishbone stitches with French knots. 17½ × 12½in.

An explanation probably lies in the moral climate of the times. Religious discussion was a favourite pastime of adults, and these texts, however dry and sombre they may seem to us, must have been familiar to the ears of children.

It is also true that there had developed a distinct tradition of sampler verses, as Mr Barrett Wendell, husband of the President of the Massachusetts Society of Colonial Dames, found out. He had long believed that the verse shown on a sampler in his possession had been composed by the father of the girl who embroidered it in 1812. The verse, of which Barrett Wendell possessed a copy in the father's handwriting, read:

Tell me, ye knowing and discerning few,
Where I may find a friend both firm and true,
Who dares stand by me in my deep distress
And then her love and friendship most express?

The answer to the question in the verse should have been 'my mother', but in this particular case domestic circumstances altered it to 'my aunt'. Barrett Wendell found, however, that the verse was listed in *American Samplers* and that a version of it had appeared on a sampler in 1718 and five more times after that—the last being in 1827. He therefore concluded that 'throughout the whole range of sampler-poetry the only trace of originality to be found is in the signature and the dates.' In fact, it is the originality of the names appearing on American samplers that is one of the most fascinating aspects of Mrs Ethel Stanwood Bolton's book. With their echoes of Ben Jonson's comedies and John Bunyan's *Pilgrim's Progress*, these quaint, lovely names attract us on every page: Content Silsbee, Temperance Mathews, Abigail Janney, Rosefair Brooks, Rocksalana Willes, Increase Githernon, Dorcas Gatcomb . . . the list is inexhaustible.

In the late 1770s, some interesting samplers were produced at Sarah Stivour's school in Salem, Massachusetts. They are notable for the very clever use of crinkly silk in long stitches often up to 5 cm long to cover areas like grass or sky, forming waves and volutes. This crinkly silk was brought from China and Japan. It was probably more readily available in Salem than in inland America, since the city was a port of some importance at the time.

Another young ladies' school in which striking samplers were produced was Polly Balch's Seminary in Providence, Rhode Island. The school had been established in 1785 by Miss Mary Balch, 'Polly, Marm Balch', who was born in Newport in 1762. The samplers that carry the hallmark of her school are probably the finest single group of American samplers. They have great social interest, too, as many represent Providence sites and buildings which no longer exist. Many samplers show the Old State Building and the old University Hall at Browne University, and one shows the First Baptist Meeting House in Providence. The samplers stand out immediately, and in spite of their individuality, they all seem related. The techniques used were also very interesting. A split-stitch background made of creamy silk, for example, is quite common and gives a soft, luminous sheen to the whole work—as can be seen in Eliza Cozzens's sampler, in which baskets of fruit appear under an arch against the silky background. It is a pity that we do not know the identity of the needlework teacher who inspired these samplers. It is clear, though, that at the end of the century she must have either died or gone away, because the design of the samplers produced after 1800 is less sure. It may be that after that date the teaching of needlework was taken over by young teachers who had themselves attended the Balch Academy.

In Pennsylvania, too, girls' schools were springing up. The earliest specimen of a school sampler from that region is that of Lydia Hoopes, made at Mrs Hollis's School, Goshen Township, Chester County in 1765. Unlike New England samplers, which were generally embroidered in silk on linen, this one is of wool on linen. It is a band sampler, without a border, and it is still in a strip shape rather than rectangular or square like contemporary New England samplers. Only two stitches are used: cross stitch, and eyelets for one of the alphabets.

Pennsylvania was an interesting area because of its mixture of cultures and traditions. A great number of its settlers had come from the British Isles to fulfil William Penn's dream of making Pennsylvania a kind of promised land for his Society of Friends, the Quakers. From 1667 onwards, Penn publicized his beloved Pennsylvania not only to Englishmen but also to Germans, Frenchmen and Dutchmen who still felt the effects of the Thirty Years War. His widely circulated pamphlets spoke of a land of opportunity where political and religious liberty was the right of every man. This must have sounded like music to the ears of German dissenters, who often suffered great hardships in a land split up into small principalities, each with its state religion, dictated by its ruler.

The Quakers believed that clothing and furnishings should be kept plain. Nevertheless, most of the samplers, canvas work, crewel work and silk embroidery made in Pennsylvania during the 18th century were done by girls of English descent. The settlers from Germany taught their daughters to do the traditional German patterns on samplers, and instilled in them their love of colour. But, as the Germans were relative new-comers in the 18th century, few examples of their needlework from before 1800 survive. Pennsylvania German samplers are, however, more truly samplers, with their scattered motifs and border patterns, than those made by girls of English descent. A good example is Regina Huebner's sampler, made in 1794. It shows alphabets, and spot motifs including dogs, birds, vases of flowers, crowns and a coach pulled by four horses. It is embroidered in silk on linen, using cross, chain, eyelet, satin and stem stitches.

Some very interesting white work samplers were produced in Pennsylvania. One example is that of R. Hughes, made in 1784 in Montgomery County in Dresden point and drawn work. At each corner of this rectangular sampler is a cut-out circle filled with needle-point lace. In the centre is a basket of flowers. Each petal of the flowers is filled with a different pattern of needle-made lace.

Dresden point was a needle-made lace which became very popular in the German city of Dresden during the last part of the 17th century and in the 18th century. It is akin to the Italian *punto tirato* and reticella, in which a lacy pattern is created by drawing out some of the threads from linen cloth and retaining others. The threads were also worked together to form a square mesh, as can be seen in the vase on the Hughes sampler. Dresden point was also embroidered in fine stitches. Dresden-type samplers were made in the Philadelphia region during the latter half of the 18th century, and the technique must have been taught to the population of the city where the German settlers would have arrived.

There is also an interesting darning sampler initialled H. C. H. and dated 1790, worked in blue and red on linen. It is difficult to guess at the origins of H.C.H. Germany is credited with the earliest darning samplers but similar work was also done in Denmark and Holland; some darning samplers were also made in England at the end of the 18th century.

In the 1790s, country scenes, animals and architectural designs appeared in Pennsylvania samplers. Crinkly silk was also being used to form the background of the picture. In 1798, Elizabeth Helms of Philadelphia embroidered a landscape showing a small house framed by trees, a wooden fence with a couple walking along it, and a shepherd and shepherdess with sheep, dogs and a very tall deer. The sampler is signed and dated neatly and the whole is enclosed in a flower-and-chain border.

Although there were many schools for girls—particularly in Philadelphia—and many samplers were produced in Pennsylvania, the products of the Stivour School or of Polly Balch's School had no 18th century counterparts there. The situation was to change drastically in the 19th century.

Unusually, this sampler was made by a boy, George Parker, when he was nine. Silk on linen. Worked in cross, satin, bullion, outline, daisy and surface satin stitches with French knots. 12 × 11in.

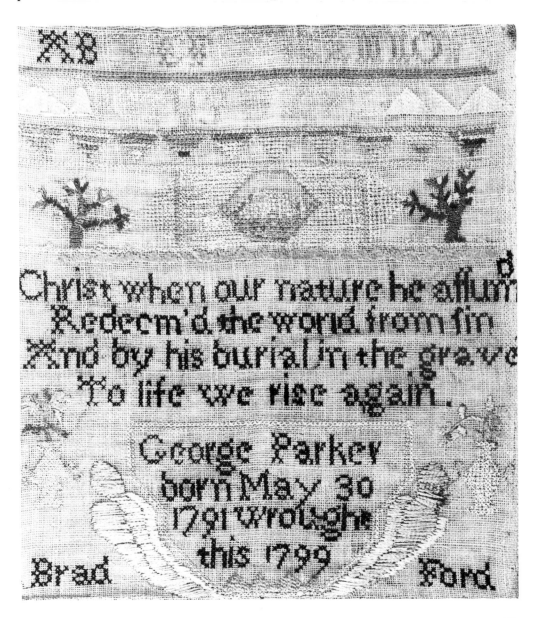

Opposite: A typical early 17th-century long, narrow sampler, 1727, embroidered with The Ten Commandments. Silk on canvas.

PRACTICAL - 18th CENTURY

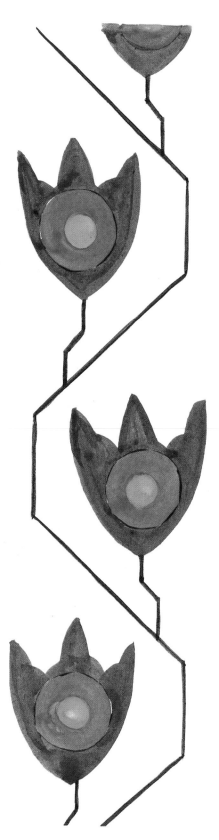

18th-century American borders worked in satin, stem and feather stitches, and French knots. They are typified by their flowing lines and glowing colours, and are easily reproduced free hand.

Birds and insects from sheets of popular prints. On samplers
these were worked in outline, satin or filling stitches with
French knots and bullion bars and loops on beetle backs,
butterfly bodies and foliage.

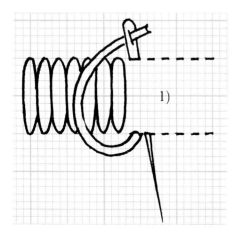

1)

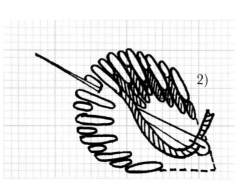

2)

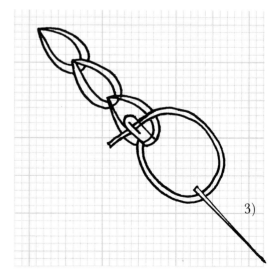

3)

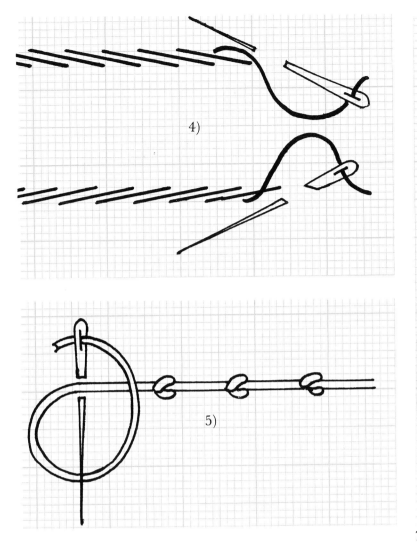

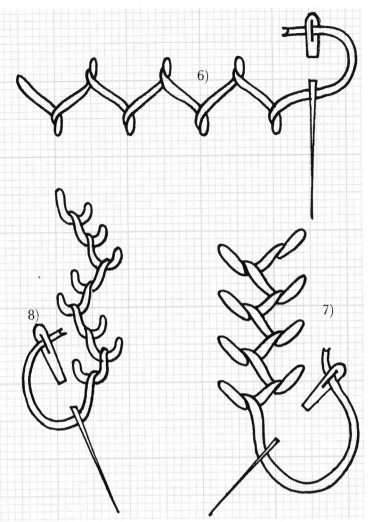

7) Cretan feather stitch. Basically a buttonhole stitch arranged zig-zag fashion with the needle angle kept at 45 degrees. Cretan feather stitch will produce a variety of effects, depending on the angle of the needle and the amount of fabric taken up on the needle. Stitches worked close together with more fabric on the needle will produce a fishbone effect with a plaited centre.

8) Double feather stitch. Buttonhole stitches worked in groups of three forming a zig-zag. The needle can be angled or upright.

9) Backstitch. Worked right to left.

1) Satin stitch.

2) Long and short satin stitch. Satin stitch worked with alternate long and short strokes. Particular attention must be paid to the direction of the stitches so that they form strong shapes and follow the natural directions of growth.

3) Chain stitch.

4) Stem or crewel stitch.
   a) Very slanting. Keep thread below and to the left. Each stitch should begin half way along the previous stitch.
   b) In this variation, the thread is kept above and will produce a finer line.

5) Coral stitch or 'snail trail', a type of chain stitch.

6) Open Cretan stitch. Cretan feather stitch worked horizontally. The needle is upright. Working closer together with larger amounts of fabric on the needle makes a filling stitch with a ribbed centre.

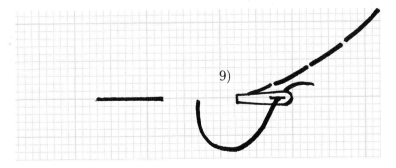

American New England motifs. Stylized treatments of plants, flowers and trees showing European folk art influences.

HOLLIE OR DRESDEN POINT

A stitch of the 18th and 19th centuries, but closely allied to the 17th-century needlepoint lace. It is also called nuns' work or holy point, because nuns were skilled in making it and it was much used for church purposes in the Middle Ages. It is a needle-made lace, and technically is a buttonhole stitch with an extra twist, worked small and closely packed. The stitches are worked in rows from left to right, taking a single thread back to the left side at the end of each row and picking it up with each stitch of the next row. The pattern is formed by missing stitches, forming holes and spaces.

First the hole is cut in the background fabric. It may be circular, square, rectangular or a strip. The edges are turned in and buttonholed evenly. This forms the ground row of the piece of lace. Rows must always be worked in the same direction, otherwise a rib effect will appear.

Hollie point patterns were simple, geometric patterns, flowers, crowns, birds, hearts.

The stitch was very popular in 18th-century Pennsylvania, probably introduced by German settlers. In Britain, hollie point continued to be made well into the 19th century, particularly on baby clothes such as robe fronts and bonnets.

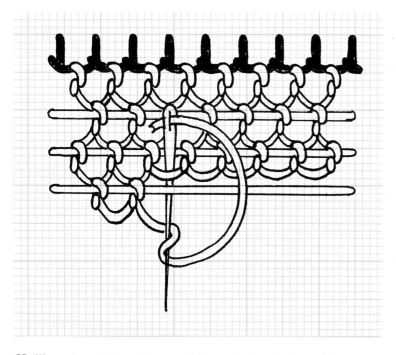

Hollie point stitch. A knotted buttonhole stitch which can be made as a detached mesh worked on a piece of fabric, or in cutwork to make a lace filling. It must be worked into a firm foundation row of ordinary buttonhole stitches. Proceed to work left to right, carrying the thread straight back to the left side to form the bar over which the next row of knotted buttonhole stitches is worked.

Traditional American motifs: house, cornucopia, pineapple, flowers.
Top right. Pastoral scene from an American sampler worked entirely in satin stitch.
Page 80. Traditional arrangements of motifs on American samplers.

79

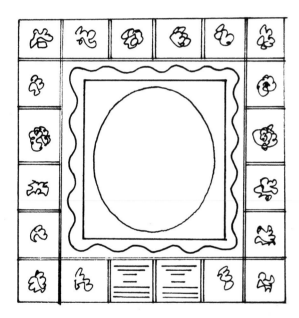

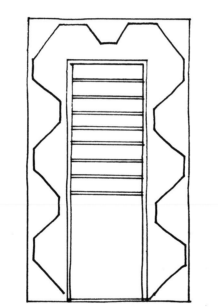

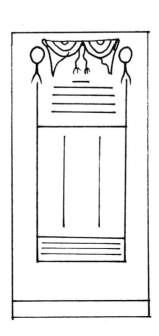

THE NINETEENTH CENTURY

Women sewing in a factory, 1856.

Work, work, work
Seam, and gusset, and band,
Band, and gusset, and seam,
Till over the buttons I fall asleep
And sew them on in a dream!

Thomas Hood: *The Song of the Shirt*

In the first half of the 19th century, before the advent of the revolutionary sewing machine, Thomas Hood's poor 'sempstress' was only one of thousands of women and children who plied their needles and thread in 'poverty, hunger and dirt', not only in the urban slums but in many country villages too. Children as young as three or four were shut up all day in 'lace schools'—overcrowded cottage rooms where they wound the bobbins and helped their elder sisters to make the lace which would earn their families a few extra pennies. In Scotland, the Ayrshire 'flowers' embroidering the fashionable white muslins from dawn to dusk were all children.

Yet these little workers were fortunate, compared with those who slaved in the coal mines, or who carried the great loads of clay required for the potteries. A knowledge of sewing and darning was often an escape route for girls, who could then aspire to enter service not just as ordinary domestics but as ladies' maids. In the 19th century, particularly after the introduction of paper patterns, a lot of women's clothes were made, or at least altered or repaired, at home, and all these tasks would be the responsibility of the maid. Even governesses were required to know how to sew, in order to teach their charges. In Mrs Gaskell's *Mary Barton*, the heroine, despite or perhaps because of her father's dislike of the leisured classes, was sure that becoming a dressmaker's apprentice would bring her several steps nearer to her goal of being a lady:

> Now while servant must often drudge and be dirty, must be known as her servant by all who visited at her master's house, a dressmaker's apprentice must (or so Mary thought) be always dressed with a certain regard to appearance; must never soil her hands, and need never redden or dirty her face with hard labour.

Such positions, however badly paid, must have looked like easy living to the girls who worked in the mills that were the back-bone of the Victorian economy. The reports of contemporary Industrial Commissions have made us familiar with the terrible conditions of work. In industrial districts, girls started work as soon as they left school, and continued until their marriage. Many women, whose husbands were ill-paid or unemployed, went on working in the mills throughout their lives, or they took in washing or hired

Detail from a very large teaching sampler, 1885. Coarse wool on wide gauge linen canvas.

themselves by the day to sew or mend. This never-ending round of toil was only briefly, if repeatedly, interrupted by childbirth.

Millions of women were paying the price for the rapid industrialization which had brought increased wealth to a new commercial and industrial aristocracy. The Cotton Lords of yesterday bought themselves mansions and brought their daughters up to be ladies, usually under the care of a governess who taught them the three R's and as many fashionable and showy accomplishments as they themselves could muster. The ideal was not so much educating the girls as fitting them for their future roles as wives and mothers. Music, a knowledge of French, embroidery and the capacity to make a thousand knick-knacks were all necessary skills in the all-important game of husband-catching.

Education for the children of the poor had been sadly neglected until well into the 19th century. There were few schools to which parents who were too poor to pay fees could send their children, male or female. The great majority of poor children received a little instruction at Sunday Schools or at Dame Schools. The latter were not supervised and their standards varied considerably. Some of these establishments may well have been run by conscientious old ladies, moved by philanthropic feelings, but many were no more than child-minders, ruthlessly exploiting a situation in which an increasing number of mothers had to work.

Even the few schools that existed were attended irregularly because of the demand for child labour. In 1825, Archdeacon Bailey, vicar of Messingham in Lincolnshire, complained that as soon as a child was capable of earning a few coppers, he was taken away from school, never to return except for a few weeks during the winter season when work was slack on the land. The same applied, of course, to children born in the industrial heart of Britain. Manufacturers had quickly discovered that many tedious, finicky operations were far better performed by the nimble fingers of children and young girls than by machines, and at a fraction of the cost.

But as the century progressed, an increasing number of people were beginning to realize the gruesome reverse side of Victorian prosperity. Their

These tiny garments were worked as 'samplers'. The smallest gloves are less than an inch long.

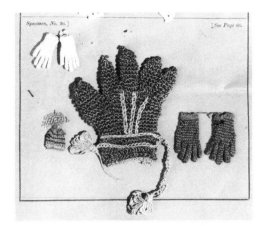

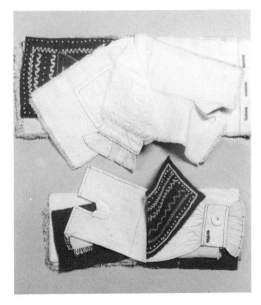

Above. A plain sewing book sampler made by Laura Slingsby in 1887. The covers are made of unbleached linen with pages in white linen for buttonholes, gathers, pleats, gussets etc., and pages in red wool for patches and stitches. It also contains a knitted page for darning.

Right. An alphabet sampler book.

attitudes, although still very much those of paternalistic do-gooders, were nevertheless an improvement over those which Hannah More professed when she established the Mendip Schools in the late 18th century. She summed up her ideas for the children of the poor as follows: 'my plan of instruction is extremely simple and limited. They learn on weekdays such coarse works as may fit them for servants. I allow of no writing for the poor. . . .' Her charges were taught knitting, spinning—and obedience. She even wrote a series of moral tales and poems to encourage this worthy quality.

Many people came to believe that elementary education should be the responsibility of the State. This theory met with great opposition from churchmen of all denominations, who felt that education without religion, or even with a religious but non-denominational approach, was no education at all, and that a government could not afford to be seen favouring one group over the other. In the 1830s and 1840s, one of the few successful educational experiments was the establishment of a government education inspectorate. Schools affiliated to the scheme received a grant, on the condition that they achieved the minimum standards laid down by government. As late as 1870, only 68 per cent of the number of children officially on the register regularly attended these schools. It is clear that, in spite of legislation limiting child-labour, the practice prevailed.

In 1870, however, an Education Act was passed which contained a commitment to a national system of elementary schools. Local Boards were elected, with the duty of levying local rates to build and administer schools. Board Schools worked under the principle of payment by results. The whole curriculum was based on a system of examination, the purpose of which was to ascertain that the school maintained a minimum standard and still qualified for grants-in-aid. This principle had the great disadvantage of fostering stereotyped instruction, learning by rote, and it encouraged large classes—head-masters had a financial interest in increasing the number of their pupils.

One look at a picture of a Victorian classroom is enough to realize the extent of the problem. Only draconian discipline and a rigid adherence to a limited curriculum could keep the system going. This affected the teaching of every subject—even that of needlework, which formed an important part of the curriculum for girls.

In Board Schools attended by children of modest means, girls were taught plain sewing rather than fancy embroidery and the samplers made at the time in these establishments reflect that approach. Many demonstrate making different kinds of seams, inserting cuffs and collars, putting in slits at the bottom of the side seams of men's shirts, making buttonholes, darning, and

'Tis not in my weak power alone,
To melt this stubborn heart of stone
My soul to change, my life to mend
Or seek to Christ, that gen'rous friend
'Tis God's own spirit from above,
Fixes our Faith inflames our Love,
And makes a life divine begin
In wretched souls long dead in sin.

Jane Crabb 1817

neatly patching linen or other fabric. These samplers also contained alphabets, especially in view of the growing fashion for marking every stitch of household or personal linen. In Mrs Gaskell's *North and South*, Mrs Thornton

All glory to the dying Lamb
And never ceasing praise
While angels live to know his name
Or saints to feel his grace

Angels! assist our mighty joys
Strike all your harps of gold
But when you raise your highest notes
His love can ne'er be told

The angels hymn his glorious name
Who lov'd and conquer'd thus
And we will likewise laud the Lamb
For he was slain for us

Elizabeth Waite
Aged 10 Years

is shown looking at her store of linen in preparation for her son's marriage:

The newly-married couple-to-be would need fresh household stocks of linen; and Mrs Thornton had clothes-basket upon clothes-basket, full of table-cloths and napkins, brought in, and began to reckon up the store. There was some confusion between what was hers and consequently marked G. H. T. (for George and Hannah Thornton), and what was her son's—bought with his money, marked with his initials. Some of those marked G. H. T. were Dutch damask of the old kind, exquisitely fine; none were like them now. Mrs Thornton stood looking at them long— they had been her pride when she was first married. Then she knit her brows, and pinched and compressed her lips tight, and carefully unpicked the G. H. She went so far as to search for the Turkey-red marking-thread to put in the new initials; but it was all used—and she had no heart to send for any more just yet.

Marking was often done by lady's maids, which explains the prominence given to marking on samplers made at schools for working-class children.

The address on Mary J. Henzell's sampler, 1883, makes her orphanage sound a very cheerless place. One hopes that the little hat and horse on the bottom cheered her up after the long rows of numbers and alphabets and suitably edifying texts.

Below. Plain sewing in book samplers was not something which rich little girls had to worry about. They practised their stitches making clothes for their dolls. Title pages and a page of designs from *Dolly's Dressmaker* published in London and Berlin.

Above. Alphabet sampler.

Throughout the century, school manuals were produced which emphasized the necessity for women to have 'a practical acquaintance with needle-work. . . . As regards plain needlework especially, this is more particularly the case with reference to females in humble life, whether with a view to domestic neatness and economy, or to profitable occupation in a pecuniary light.' These principles were stated in the preface to *Plain Needlework in all its branches*, published in 1849 for use in the National Industrial School of the Holy Trinity, at Finchley. Step by step, by means of questions and answers, it took the young girl through all the basic sewing techniques.

The same book set out the following curriculum for Class II of the National Industrial Schools:

4. Back Stitch
5. Chain ..
6. Darning ..
7. Basting Stitch
8. Herring-bone ..
9. Marking Stitch
10 Overcast ..
11 Button-hole ..

Right. Nine squares joined together with white linen tape. The joins are hidden with dark blue satin ribbon decorated with pink silk thread. Each square is brightly embroidered in darning, needle lace and knitted darning stitches using coloured silk. The piece is mounted on thick paper. Early 19th century, 6¼in. square.

Son of God thy blessing grant
Still supply my ev'ry want
Tree of Life thine influence shed
With thy sap my spirit feed

Tend'rest branch alas am I
Wither without thee and die
Weak as helpless infancy
O confirm my soul in thee

All my hopes on thee depend
Love me save me to the end
Give me the continuing grace
Take the everlasting praise

Elisabeth Barratt Her Work
Finished October the 30 1824

Elisabeth Barratt's sampler, finished in 1824.

12. Oeillet-hole ··

These 12 stitches are first taught and practised upon the Third-Class Sampler, and then they are all done upon the Second Class Sampler.

The Alphabet, Figures, Etc. are to be done on the Second Class Sampler according to the pattern, to which each girl is to add the Initials of her Christian and Surname, and the Year in Figures.
Sew patchwork with the different Seamstitches.
Hem and Mark dusters, etc.
Hem and Seam aprons and pinafores.

This type of school sampler fulfilled a definite purpose, as did other school products such as Maria Nicholls's sampler, worked at St Matthew's School

This unusual sampler depicts the four seasons of the year with scenes of country life. Isabella Francis Hatcher, 31st March 1827.

in 1846 and consisting of a daunting long division sum, embroidered in minute cross-stitch on tiffany. The tradition, born in the previous century, of embroidering long passages from the Bible, or a prayer in black silk, still continued: the three Brontë sisters produced samplers of this kind. At the time, Anne was ten years old, Charlotte thirteen and Emily eleven. Anne's, illustrated here, consisted of an extract from Proverbs, 26 lines of closely set lettering, which she worked in 1830. The sampler in itself is of little aesthetic interest. It is worked in black silk on rough cloth and shows a singular lack

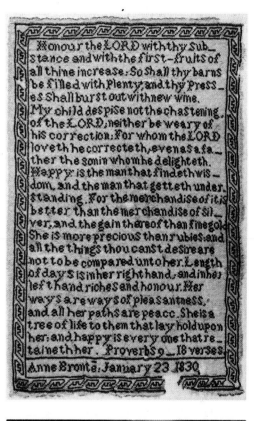

A useful way to remember compound division. Worked by Maria Nicholls at St Matthew's School in 1846. Cross stitch on tiffany.

The Brontë sisters cannot have had much fun stitching samplers like this one by Anne. They had to sew them with Psalms and texts from the Bible.

of ornament. Charlotte's and Emily's samplers were identical in all but the choice of text. The samplers' very drabness conveys the gloomy atmosphere in which the sisters lived.

The style of samplers was gradually changing: they were becoming purely decorative objects to be prettily framed and hung on the parlour wall. At the beginning of the century, the sampler still possessed a degree of originality and spontaneity, and it differed little from its predecessors of the late 18th century. Slowly, however, the range of stitches in use diminished, until samplers were literally equated with the cross-stitch alone. Designs became stereotyped, and prim symmetry became the rule. Alphabets were still embroidered on the sampler, but if a few letters remained after filling the line or lines, the letters were simply left out. There was also far less variety in the motifs. Houses and gardens are far less elaborately treated. Animals, birds and trees had to balance neatly. A verse was inserted and flanked by spot motifs, but these both had to mirror each other, for the sake of perfect symmetry.

The fabric used was woollen tammy, which became as common as linen. As a result, 19th century samplers are in a worse state of preservation than much earlier ones, which were done on linen and therefore remained impervious to moths. The embroidery was done chiefly in silk and wool, or silk

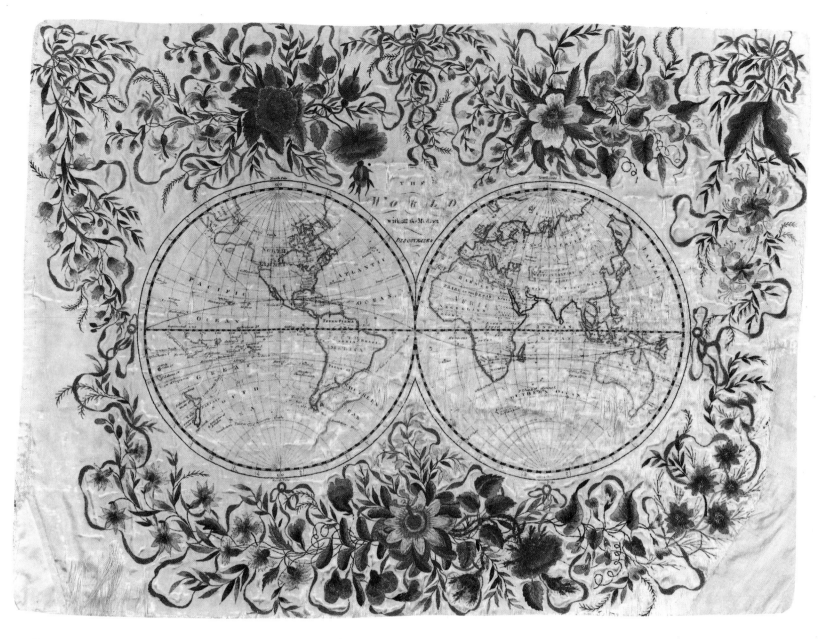

This elegant map sampler was printed in black on satin 'THE WORLD with all the Modern DISCOVERIES' and then framed within a floral border. Coloured silk on satin. Worked in satin, stem, long and short and straight stitches and French knots. *c*1800. $18\frac{1}{8} \times 26$in.

Branwell Brontë's portrait of his three sisters.

and cotton, but some samplers were worked entirely in a single type of thread: silk, wool, linen or cotton. The colours chosen appear today to be very glaring; they must have been even more so when the thread was new. The first of the synthetic aniline dyes, mauve was prepared by W. H. Perkin in 1856 and was followed by others which made available bright viridian, brilliant scarlets and magentas. In a world where people were almost constantly wearing black because they were never for long out of mourning, bright colours, such as the gorgeous hues seen on Indian and other Oriental fabrics, were highly desirable. But early aniline dyes failed to reproduce the subtleties of the exotic colours they sought to imitate, and this, together with the craze for Berlin woolwork, contributed to the decline of the sampler. As A. F. Kendrick wrote in his *History of English Needlework*, 'Its end is witnessed with the regret that is inseparable from the spectacle of something useful lapsing into something merely ornamental.'

The decline of the sampler was not an isolated phenomenon. Embroidery, and the decorative arts in general, suffered from the passion for excessive decoration. Blinded by the glaring colours of Berlin wool-work, women ignored the beauty and purity of embroidery done in earlier years.

The Berlin designs exemplified the 19th century love of the literal. The patterns, which formed vignettes or complete scenes, are sharply three-dimensional, imitating the technique of contemporary painters, who used a large numbers of colours to produce effects of light and shade. Popular paintings were, in fact, adapted to be copied, square by square on the canvas, like painting by numbers.

All manner of work—chairs, footstools, curtains, cushions, bell-pulls—was covered in the ubiquitous Berlin work. Common subjects were floral or geometrical motifs, cats and dogs (including Queen Victoria's King Charles spaniel, 'Dash') and portraits of the Royal Family – 'Bertie', the future Prince of Wales, was the great favourite. Even a contemporary article in *The Girl's Own Annual* pointed out the irony of such a portrait being mounted flat on a footstool. Obviously, Her Majesty's loyal subjects saw nothing wrong in trampling the Prince of Wales underfoot.

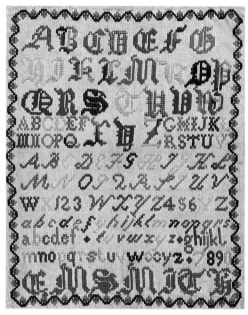

A full range of Berlin colours. Late 19th-century alphabet sampler.

Ann Schofield's large red house surrounded by plants, birds, dogs and a butterfly is a charming example of the more stylised 19th-century sampler. Wool on canvas, 1848.

An ark of animals worked in cross stitch on canvas, 1887.

Berlin wool, or zephyr yarns, were manufactured in Germany at Gotha, and then dyed in Berlin. Also from Berlin came the patterns, printed on squared paper which could be copied in cross or tent stitch on canvas. A Berlin print-seller named Philipson is credited with having published, in 1804 or 1805, the first coloured design on squared paper for needlework. These designs were imported into England by leading publishers such as Ackermann, and their popularity was such that by 1840 no less than 14,000 different designs for wool work had been published.

In 1831, Mr Wilks, the owner of London's leading needlework supplies shop, began importing large quantities of the patterns direct from Berlin, together with the materials for working them. The *Illustrated London News* for 14th December 1844 announced that Wilks's Warehouse, 18b Regent St., had a superb assortment of wools of all kinds, plain, chiné and shaded, including the four-thread Berlin wool, and the Imperial light-thread or double Berlin:

> All these wools, spun especially for this house, are remarkable for their quality, and present, beyond all comparison, the largest and best assorted stock in the kingdom. Berlin patterns and every other article, whether of British or Foreign Manufacture, used in Decorative Needlework.

This King Charles spaniel is worked in a kind of looped stitch, cut very short and forming a thick pile. The background is Berlin woolwork done in cross stitch. This work is typical and may have represented Queen Victoria's spaniel, Dash.

A few years later, Mr Wilks was probably selling a new type of sampler, worked not by children but by professional needlewomen as guides for amateurs. These samplers were on long, narrow strips of canvas, the edges often bound with silk ribbon. Blocks of patterns and floral motifs were worked in simple cross-stitch. But there was also a wide variety of other stitches. There were, for example, Hungarian, Florentine and brick stitches, and canvas lace work in which the open net ground of the lace was worked in silk and the close parts of the pattern in cross-stitch with thicker silk, or

Wm. Briggs & Co. were responsible for inventing the Hot Iron Transfer for embroidery designs. While such easy methods somewhat detracted from original design, their period charm is nonetheless very attractive.. This example is from one of their catalogues produced in the 1880s.

A strip sampler of Bargello patterns, late
19th century.

Solomon's Temple in all its glory worked by Sarah Millington in 1849. Her vision of the temple looks remarkably like a Victorian Town Hall.

in four-thread Berlin wool. There was also considerable variety among cross-stitches—such as the leviathan or railway stitch, which was worked on four squares of canvas instead of one. Another example was the perspective stitch, which gave a *trompe l'œil* effect. The *Illuminated Book of Needlework* (1847) lists 32 different canvas stitches, with such picturesque names as Windsor, Hohenlinden and Sutherland.

Various types of canvas were also used. Berlin or silk canvas, the most expensive, was made of a very fine mesh and needed no grounding. It was considered suitable for small, delicate patterns, which were often worked in silk, chenille or beads. It was available in three colours: black, white, or pearl white.

German cotton canvas was the cheapest. To make counting easier, every tenth thread was yellow. French canvas had a square, even mesh, and was pleasant to work on. Penelope canvas had threads in sets of four. All these canvases came in different grades. By 1851, canvas could also be bought with the design printed in the appropriate colours. By 1880, various mechanical aids to make cross-stitch embroidery still easier were introduced—notably the new machine-perforated batswing cloth, made by Messrs Biggs of Manchester, which did away with the tedious job of counting threads.

Sam Beeton, the husband of the famous Mrs Beeton, edited several popular women's magazines and was a very successful publisher. When still quite young, he made a fortune by being the first British publisher of Harriet Beecher Stowe's anti-slavery novel, *Uncle Tom's Cabin*. He made a second fortune from launching the *Boys' Own Paper*, one of the first magazines to capture the juvenile market; and a third by pioneering a great number of women's periodicals such as *The Queen* and *The Englishwoman's Domestic Magazine*, together with his wife's classic cookery book, which he largely inspired and which is still in print today.

Sam Beeton was also an innovator in the publication of paper patterns for dressmaking. By a special arrangement with M. Adolphe Goubaud, publisher of *Le Moniteur des Modes* in Paris, French fashion plates were sent to

Sam Beeton, husband of the famed Mrs Beeton and publisher of *Beeton's Book of Needlework*.

St Mary's Girls' National School. The splendid pink building framed in a strawberry border is unfinished. The stitches include cross, tent, satin and eyelet. Second half of the 19th century.

London every week; then Isabella Beeton translated and edited Mme Goubaud's descriptions; and finally a young assistant, Mr Wheeldon, produced the folded paper patterns, which were stuck into the magazine together with a hand-coloured embroidery pattern. The system functioned efficiently, even through the siege of Paris in 1871, when the fashion newsletter had to be sent out of the capital by balloon.

Sam Beeton was quick to realize the financial potentialities of the Berlin work craze, and he had the idea of inserting coloured paper guides which his readers could reproduce themselves on canvas. In 1844, he declared in *The Young Ladies' Journal*:

> we continue to supply our readers with as many designs in strips and borders in Berlin work as possible because we are assured of their utility. It is quite easy to be working these strips either on the beach or in the garden as they may be rolled up and enclosed in neat little Holland bags. . . . When worked they may be used for so many purposes—cushions, stools, borders or table covers and travelling bags etc.

Sam Beeton was not alone in his enthusiasm for this type of work. Ladies' magazines on both sides of the Atlantic printed Berlin work patterns. Other publishers produced greeting cards, bookmarks, needlebooks and larger edifying mottoes or heraldic symbols, all printed on perforated card to be worked in silk or Berlin wool.

The Arts and Crafts Movement was a reaction to the plethora of factory-made goods and tried to bring back good design and craftsmanship. William Morris and others tried to bring about a revival in embroidery. Their efforts, however, had little effect on the general public and certainly did not bring back the sampler. By this time most embroidery, and much plain sewing, had become nothing more than a pleasant parlour pastime. For all practical purposes machines had taken over. In New York, Isaac Singer had produced the first successful sewing machine, while the first embroidery machine,

Ships in harbour fill the bottom of Euphemia Doig's sampler, made in 1814. The verse is v. 13 of the Scottish Metrical version of Psalm CIII. Coloured woollen threads on wool, cross, back, satin and eyelet stitch. 13 × 12¾in.

Left. This Welsh sampler was made by Mary Lewis in 1824.

Right. Eliza Priscilla Killick's sampler with alphabets and numerals also contains a verse from Isaiah and was made at Christ Church School, Tunbridge Wells, Kent in 1867.

invented in 1828 by Monsieur Heilman of Mulhouse, had been so improved that, with the use of silks dyed in graduated tints, *ombre* silks, effects could be achieved which resembled hand embroidery. It would take many years before embroiderers rediscovered the potentials of their craft.

My Thirteenth Year of Age is Past
O Lord Point Me The Way
To Anchor in Thy Narrow Path
And Never From It Stray
(Hannah Harforth's sampler, 1808)

Lydia Smith's sampler, dated March 29, 1803, comes from the eastern part of Massachusetts. The faces and hands of the people are painted, and traces of the original drawing in pencil are visible. Silk on cotton. Many of the stitches are long floating ones measuring $1\frac{1}{2}$in. or more in length, a feature of American samplers. Other stitches are stem, satin, chain, surface, satin and wishbone with cross stitch. 18 × 29in.

In the late 18th century, the variety of stitches used on American samplers appeared to be diminishing. This tendency was confirmed in the new century. By far the most popular stitch used in surviving 19th-century specimens is the cross-stitch. In the 18th century, samplers had also shown great originality and inventiveness in their use of materials other than silk threads. Around 1795, Patty Cogeshall of Bristol, Rhode Island, made a sampler that shows the chariot of Cupid and Venus. She enhanced her embroidery with metal thread, purl-stitched edgings, spangles and striking black-worked borders. Small figures and a profusion of flowers are finely arranged in a border, the background of which is worked all over with black floss silk. The cartouche containing Patty's name and her date of birth is similarly filled, but with shimmering white silk.

The metal thread and other embellishments in Patty's work, far from making it look gaudy, enhance the design. But this practice was discontinued in the 19th century. The linen fabric also sometimes gave place to linsey-woolsey. In 1800, some examples of crossband samplers were still being made, but these gradually died out and were replaced by the pictorial variety already encountered in the late 18th century.

Judging from surviving specimens, very large numbers of samplers were worked during the early years of the new century. But as the years went by, the originality, the workmanship and even the number of samplers produced diminished. Soon after 1830, what most authorities regard as the great period of the American sampler ended. In England and in most European countries, too, a similar decline was taking place. In America, however, the end, though very sudden, came much later than in England. This was probably due to the scarcity of pattern books in America, which meant that, for their inspiration, children had to turn largely to every-day elements or

Opposite. Mary Richardson's sampler (1783), worked when she was 12, was probably made at Sarah Stivour's School. The verse reads:
'Mary Richardson is my name and With My Needle I did the same and if my skil *[sic]* had been better I would have mended every letter. This needle work of mine can tell when a child is learned well. By my parents I was tought *[sic]* not to spend my time for nought.'

Mary Richardson Is My Name And With My
Needle Did The Same And If My Skil Had Been
Better I Would Have Mended Every Letter
This Needle Work Of Mine Can Tell When A
Child Is Learned Well By My Parants I Was
Tought Not To Spend My Time For Nought

'Hannah Gale wrought this in the 11th year of her age 1801 Haverhill County Essex.' Polychrome silk thread on natural canvas. 14 × 17¾in.

to seek the advice of an older person. Although the practice of making samplers at school was widespread, many of these schools' reputations were founded largely on the originality of the needlework they taught—a lady-like accomplishment which had become a great status symbol. Each school had developed its own particular style, instead of relying on textbook instructions, as was the case in England.

Some of the best school samplers in the 19th century were made in Pennsylvania. These often gave the names of the teachers concerned. One of the most famous was Mrs Leah Meguier, who had a school at Harrisburg in the early 1800s and was certainly the same person who, as Miss Leah Galligher, had run a school in Lancaster around 1797. In evidence, we have a sampler made by Sara Holsworth in 1799 in Lancaster, naming Leah Galligher as her teacher. Her sampler is very similar to that of Elizabeth Finney, embroidered in 1807 at Mrs Leah Meguier's school in Harrisburg. The styles are both quite striking. Both samplers have a highly unusual border, which is quite wide and divided into squares, each containing a different motif. Both embroideries contain a very wide range of stitches. Sarah Holsworth made this border on three sides of her sampler, the bottom section representing the Lancaster Poorhouse. Elizabeth Finney's sampler is a much more fancy effort, with an all-round border, divided into 22 squares filled with similar conventionalized strawberries, baskets of fruit, hearts and trees as well as small human figures and birds. Inside this outer border is a kind of secondary border, quite narrow, containing a garland of flowers with the leaves very effectively worked in bullion stitch. The centre of the sampler shows a courting couple with another woman sitting under a willow tree—a common feature in Pennsylvania samplers—holding a garland of flowers. The man's coat buttons are simulated with sequins as are

Lydia Fawcett was a Quaker child, born in 1822. Sampler in silk on linen. Worked in cross, rococo, satin and slanting gobelin stitch.

those on the girls' dresses. The faces, always very difficult to reproduce in embroidery, are delicately painted on the muslin ground. This sampler, which is thought to be the most elaborate found in Pennsylvania must have been an object of pride for both pupil and teacher. It is carefully framed with a wide crimson ribbon which is further embellished by gold lace.

Another product of the Leah Meguier's School was Ann E. Kelly's sampler, worked in 1825. It also has the border divided into square sections. But what is most interesting is the way in which she has worked the face of the woman who offers a sacrifice on an altar: she has inserted the painted face under the muslin background. Of all the attempts at representing the human face on samplers—embroidering it, painting it with water colours or oil paint, painting it on paper and sticking to the cloth—Ann Kelly's solution is probably the most successful. The effect is quite ethereal, but could, of course, only be achieved with a very fine and diaphanous fabric.

Much more sober but quite distinctive samplers were produced at the Westtown Boarding School in Westtown Township, Chester County, which had opened in 1799. This establishment was under the supervision of the Philadelphia Yearly Meeting of the Society of Friends. An extract of their information sheet for the parents of prospective pupils, as described in Helen

Above left. 'Margaret Moss aged 11 year 1825'. A sampler from Pennsylvania, worked in silk on open mesh cotton. Satin, surface satin, cross, chain and eyelet stitches. 27¼ × 26in.

Above right. The face of the woman on Ann E. Kelley's sampler, made in 1826, is painted on paper and then pasted to the underside of the fabric. The sampler was made at Mrs Leah Meguier's school in Harrisburg, Pennsylvania, with the edges typically bound in white satin damask. 18 × 18in.

In Sarah Yeakel's sampler, 1806, some of the details on the sheep are in black ink. Cotton on open mesh, coarse linen. 16¾ × 21¾in.

The village of North Branford, Connecticut is depicted at the bottom of Sophia Stevens Smith's sampler, 1818. The church, centre right, burned down in 1910. The horses and the hills in the background are painted on the fabric and traces of the original drawing can still be seen. Silk on cotton. 17¼ × 23½in.

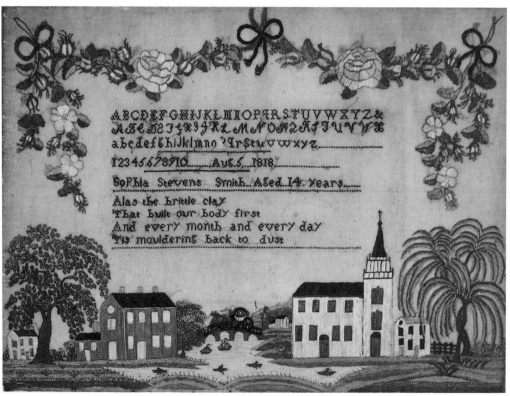

Opposite, left. A memorial picture made by Mary Bechler in 1838. Human hair is embroidered in loosely worked satin stitch on the head of each of the figures. 17 × 19in.

Opposite, right. Mary French credits her teacher, Mary N. Moody in this sampler made in 1826. Silk on linen. Worked in cross, satin, outline, buttonhole, herringbone and upright Gobelin. 17¾ × 17¾in.

G. Hole's *Westtown through the Years*, does indicate that the school was not interested in teaching elaborate, fancy embroidery on the Meguier lines:

> Two weeks in six are spent in the sewing school, from which the girls go to reading and writing classes as usual, but during the rest of the time they are busy with the needle. Plain sewing comes first, and darning as well. A piece twelve by eight inches must be so perfectly darned that the mending can scarcely be distinguished from the original material. This examination passed, the students undertake the complex embroidery of spectacle cases, globes representing the earth, and samplers with beautifully stitched designs bordering alphabets and moral sentiments, usually in poetry. Some of the more proficient are allowed to stitch views of the School, to be framed and exhibited as pictures, but this, as well as the making of elaborate samplers is frowned on by the Committee as 'superfluous' and to be discouraged.

Hannah Poole's sampler, made in 1813, is a good example of Westtown's 'no nonsense' type of work. It is a darning sampler with seven squares, each containing a different darning pattern, worked in white on grey-blue linen. Also embroidered are Hannah's name, that of the school and the date in cross-stitch. Many other Westtown samplers consisted of alphabets encircled by a very plain vine pattern. The shades of silk used are quite muted; most of the samplers are simply in black silk on linen.

Very few samplers showing the actual school building have survived, which would indicate that pupils were seldom encouraged to branch out into such 'frivolous' work. A few celestial and terrestrial globes were made. These could in some ways be related to the globe and map samplers that reached such popularity in England during the 18th century. There is little actual embroidery on the globes. The lines of longitude and latitude are simply couched down, and boundaries are often worked in outline stitch. Names of countries, oceans or constellations are painted in black on the silk ground.

The rarity of map samplers is perhaps explained by the sheer size of America. It would have been a very difficult task to stitch the whole country. There is, however, one example of a map of the United States, made in 1813 by Mary H. Walter at Mrs Given's School in Chester County. It is embroidered on silk in a variety of stitches. Around 1840, a map of Pennsylvania was made by an anonymous girl, probably at school. It is composed entirely of needle-made lace on a lacy ground. Each county is represented by a different pattern.

One very interesting type of 19th-century sampler is the family record. Some were made during the last years of the 18th century, but their popularity really reached its peak during the 19th century. They are usually inscribed 'Genealogy', 'Family Register' or 'Family Record'. Some are very plain, with the inscription worked in cross-stitch and only a narrow border for decoration. Others are as decorative as they are informative. The best have pillars on each side and an arch across the top, further decorated by garlands of flowers. There are also examples of genealogical trees, with the names of family members inscribed in 'fruits' hanging from branches.

Family record samplers have a certain poignancy. They show us how precarious life still was in the 19th century. Infant mortality was high. In a sampler dated 1824, for example, Catherine Meach, records the death of

This family record was stitched by M.L. Towner, a Baptist child in Patterson, New York in 1835. It traces the family from 1784 to 1828. Silk on linen. Worked in cross, satin, closed herringbone, laid work, rococo (queen), tent stitches. $16\frac{1}{4} \times 16\frac{3}{4}$ in.

four small brothers and sisters, 'all removed from this world in the course of five months'. The frequency of men's second, and even third, marriages gives us an idea of the strain put on women's health by repeated childbirth. Jane E. Blatchford's sampler, made in 1814, records the births of seventeen children in twenty-three years. Little wonder that children were so conscious of death. Betsy Cook inscribed this verse on her sampler:

> This work in hand my friends may have,
> When I am dead and laid in grave.

This verse was a very common one, but she emphasized the gloomy character of the piece by embroidering a tombstone carrying her initials and shaded by the usual willow tree.

A message of gloom was also appropriate for the art of the sampler. Although a few were still made after 1830, the sparkle and spontaneity was gone and they were only shadows of their predecessors. The 20th century has seen a revival of interest in the sampler, both as a collector's item and as a pastime, but the comparison between the few examples of modern American samplers with the rich heritage of the past cannot help but be painful.

Sampler by Betsey Ellis Hutchinson, 1831. Ivory and blue are the predominant colours. Silk on linen. 17 × 16½in.

PRACTICAL - 19th CENTURY

19TH CENTURY NEEDLECRAFT

From the evidence of samplers alone, it would appear that during the 19th century domestic embroidery skills dwindled to become little more than 'sewing-by-numbers' from printed patterns in the ubiquitous cross stich. Exceptions are the darning and plain sewing samplers, and the long strip Berlin work samplers. These were repertoires of patterns and stitches with a practical purpose; they usually show great skill. It is often argued that the wide distribution of ready-made patterns led to a lack of originality or individuality among embroiderers and brought about the decline of the sampler, yet this copying could be said to be in the sampler tradition. Foreign pattern books provided most of the early designs which were subsequently copied from one another. Much of the interest of older samplers was in the rearrangement of familiar, borrowed motifs and their individual interpretations. In the 19th century, printed patterns were worked out to the last detail, and this did probably discourage inventiveness.

Curiously, despite the rather stereotyped range of motifs and the paucity of stitches, it is in the ordinary Victorian sampler that the personality of the embroiderer often comes through. As the worker was usually quite a young child, the choice of the moralizing text was probably set by an adult, but the arrangement of houses, people or potted plants; the prominence of man, age and date seem to be the child's own personal touch and render these samplers engagingly personal and, perhaps deceptively, spontaneous.

Not all the motifs were taken from Berlin patterns. Many of the angels, birds and animals which were particularly popular are common continental folk patterns, whilst others in a freer style, particularly insects and flowers, appear to come from sheets of popular prints and scrapbooks.

Berlin woolwork, because of its enormous impact, tends to overshadow the popularity of other crafts, the products of which adorned even modest Victorian houses. There was suddenly a mass of handwork a girl could do. 'Fancy work' was born, and magazines, which regularly suggested new uses for raffia, paper and cardboard, glue, beads, wire, paint and yarns of all sorts, became extremely successful. The weekly or monthly quest for novelty seems at times to have stretched the ingenuity of the editors to the limit or even beyond. However, apart from the Watteau shaped palm baskets and pom-pom fly rests, these magazines were chiefly responsible for the revival of a large range of needlework skills. One of the most important was knitting. It had once been a guild craft, but had declined with the industrial revolution to become, except in certain fishing communities, little more than a cottage pursuit. With fast-dyed, plied knitting yarns available in consistent quality, it became a popular handicraft, and was high fashion by the turn of the century.

Early magazines included the *Ladies' Album of Fancy Work* (1849) which taught embroidery, netting, knitting and crochet, but perhaps the best known is what became *Weldon's Practical Needlework*. It offered regular sections on crochet, tatting, knitting and embroidery. The contents of *Weldon's* ranged from practical clothing like socks and petticoats, through toys and napery, to church bazaar novelties such as crinkled tissue paper work. The magazine was extremely well illustrated with detailed engravings.

Paper held a particular place as a Victorian 'modern' material. It became cheaper to produce during the 1870s. Because only scissors and glue were needed, paper was seized on as a handicraft material. It could be folded, pierced, cut, coloured and crushed to become pin-prick pictures, washstand splashbacks, candle and lampshades, valentines and Christmas garlands, and it could also be sewn and embroidered. Texts and samplers are found worked on mechanically perforated card, specially made for the purpose.

Printed cotton textiles also became relatively cheap, and patchwork, which had grown out of the need to use up or reuse cloth enjoyed renewed popularity. Special prints could even be bought for centrepieces and borders. It is paradoxical that if industry made the basic materials cheaper and more available, it also created an enormous amateur interest in handmade goods.

Opposite page. Adam and Eve motif. Common on samplers on both sides of the Atlantic during the 18th and 19th centuries.

Pages 110 and 111. Other traditional spot motifs. Some probably stemmed from heraldry while others derived from popular prints.

Page 112. Schematic trees and bushes reflecting the earlier garden fashion for topiary. Traditionally worked in cross or rococo stitch, these motifs can also be worked in almost any counted thread stitch, including eyelet, satin, gobelin leviathan, long armed cross or pulled thread stitches.

Page 113. Potted plants. In the 19th century, plants were shown in pots and vases rather than growing in the ground.

Page 114. Stylized birds and flowers enclosed in geometrical shapes. This type of pattern appeared between 1790 and 1810. Worked in monochrome black, brown or white thread. It appeared on English and American samplers. A common source of printed pattern is almost certain, as details differ hardly at all. These motifs still appeared after 1810, but without their enclosing borders.

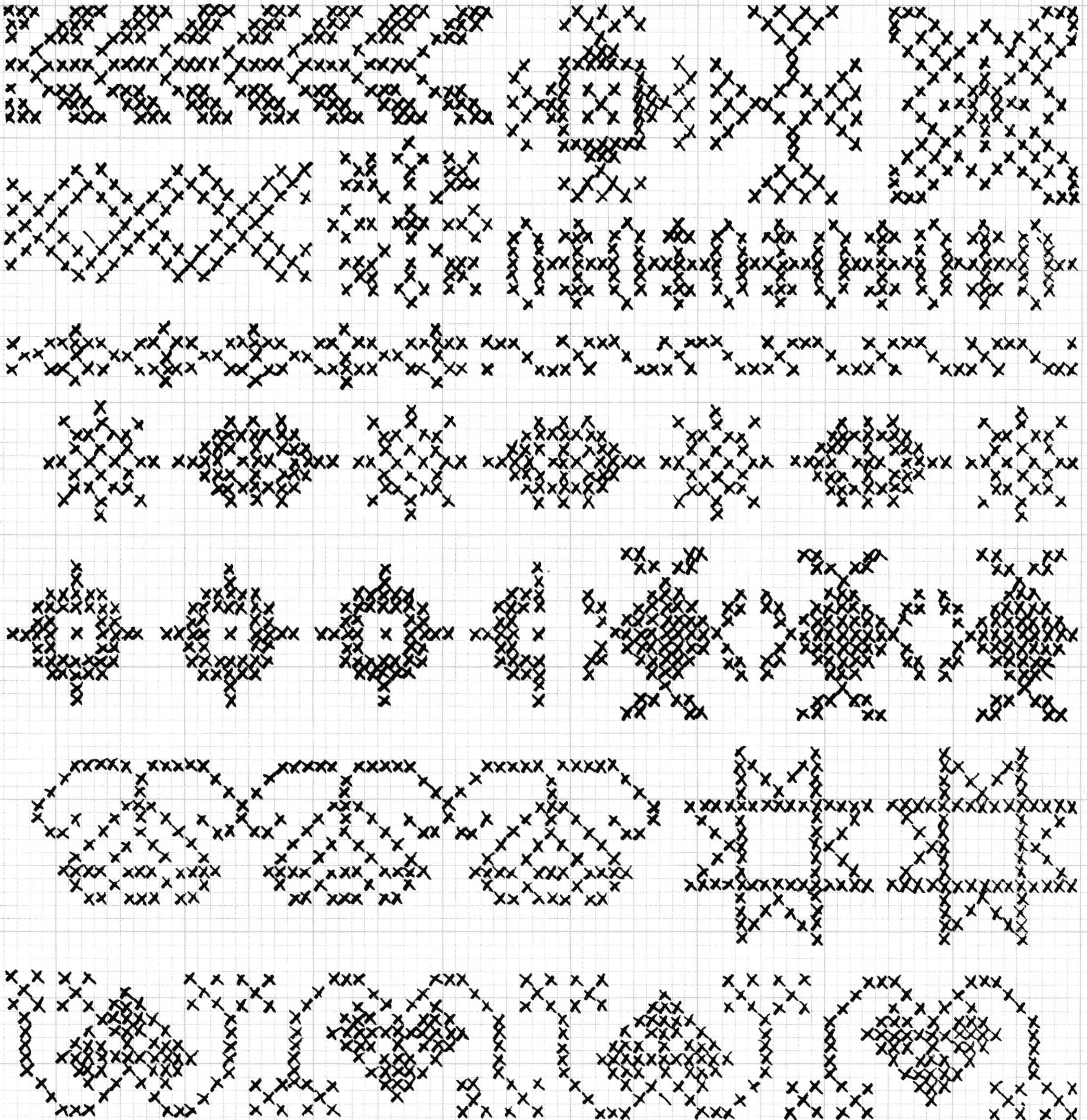

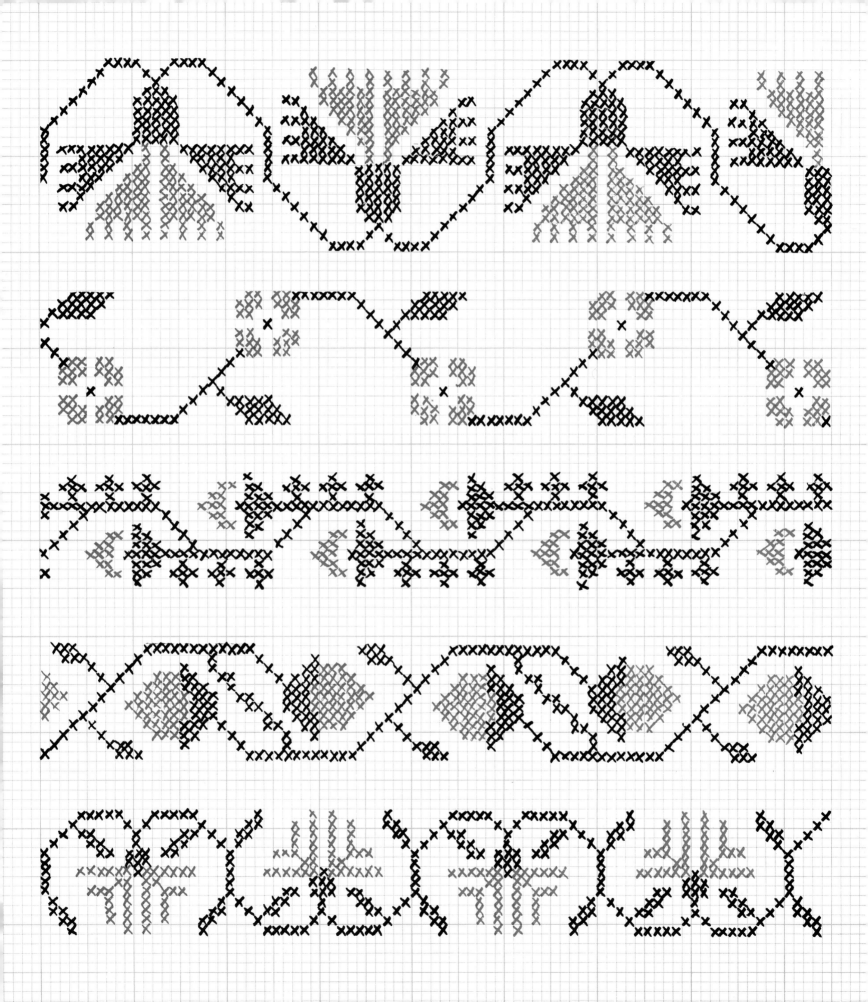

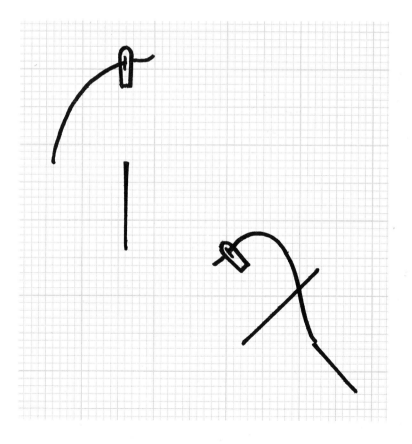

Two 19th-century American sampler designs. American samplers were much more freely drawn and pictorial than British ones.

Page 115. Cross stitch bands. These were used to divide pattern areas in samplers and fill in odd spaces.

Page 116. Arcaded borders. Carnation, wild roses, honeysuckle and flower buds.

Cross stitch. Also known as marking stitch and sampler stitch, because of its wide use in marking linen and as the stitch mainly used on 19th-century samplers.

BERLIN WORK

INSTRUCTIONS.

———◆———

BERLIN WORK includes every kind of stitch which is made upon canvas with wool, silk, or beads. The principal stitches used are common cross stitch, Gobelin stitch, leviathan stitch, raised or velvet stitch, tent stitch, and others. The materials and needle must always be carefully chosen of a corresponding size. For common cross stitch and raised stitch Penelope canvas must be used; for small articles, such as slippers, bags, or borders, single Berlin wool is preferable; for larger ones fleecy wool or double Berlin wool (the latter, however, is much more expensive). For Gobelin stitch and tent stitch undivided canvas (not Penelope) is required. Purse silk is often used for the latter; it is more brilliant than floss silk or filoselle. Floss silk is generally used for other stitches because it covers the thread of the canvas better than purse silk; it is, however, often replaced by filoselle, which is a much cheaper material. Moss wool is hardly ever used. Before beginning to work upon a piece of canvas the raw edges must be hemmed or sewn over

with wool. Care must be taken not to crumple the canvas in the course of the work. It is best to roll one end of the canvas upon a round piece of deal while the other end is kept down upon the table with a lead cushion. Handsome artistic patterns should always be worked in a frame. When you undertake to work a large pattern begin in the centre, and complete one half before you commence the other. Always work the stitches in the same direction, from the top downwards—this is very essential to the beauty and regularity of the pattern.

Always begin with the colour which is used the oftenest; those colours that lose their dye in working must be put in last. When the pattern is finished begin the grounding. The wool must not be drawn too tightly, otherwise the threads of the canvas appear. If the wool is too coarse for the canvas, one long stitch is to be made from left to right as far as the particular colour is to be worked, and over this long stitch, cross back in the usual way.

The plainest stitch in Berlin wool work is the common cross stitch; illustrations 577 to 584 show varieties of the same.

We now proceed in the following pages to show, by description in writing and by most careful illustration, all the stitches which are used in Berlin Work. These are numerous, but neither too great in number nor too simple or too elaborate in execution for those who aspire to become Berlin workers.

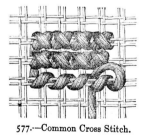
577.—Common Cross Stitch.

578.—Long Cross Stitch.

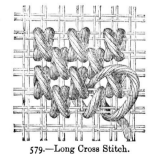
579.—Long Cross Stitch.

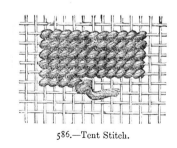
586.—Tent Stitch.

Berlin work: instructions and illustrations of stitches from *Beeton's Book of Needlework.*

118

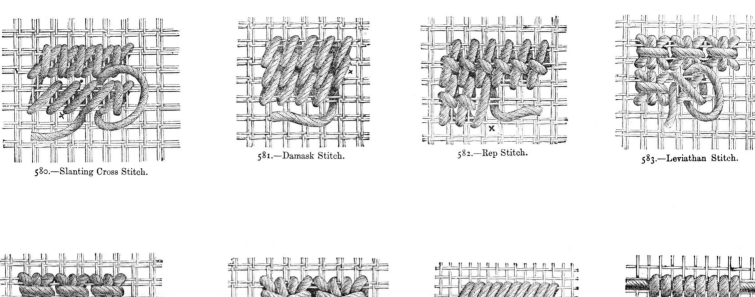

580.—Slanting Cross Stitch.

581.—Damask Stitch.

582.—Rep Stitch.

583.—Leviathan Stitch.

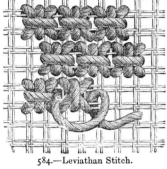

584.—Leviathan Stitch.

585.—Double Leviathan Stitch.

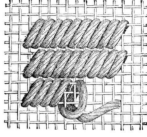

587.—Slanting Gobelin Stitch.

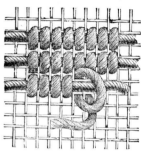

588.—Straight Gobelin Stitch.

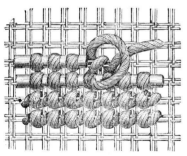

589.—Raised or Velvet Stitch.

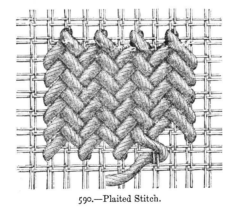

590.—Plaited Stitch.

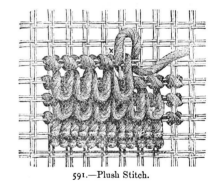

591.—Plush Stitch.

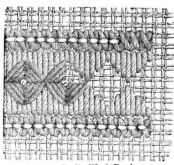

592.—Berlin Work Border.

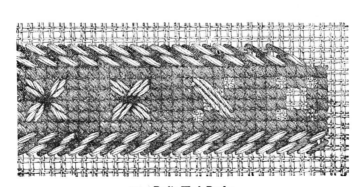

593.—Berlin Work Border.

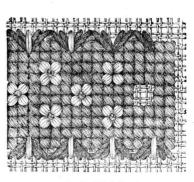

594.—Berlin Work Border.

THE TWENTIETH CENTURY

World War I precipitated millions of women into jobs and increased their responsibilities, changing their aspirations and their expectations of life. They demanded and obtained some political rights, better education and a greater part in the social and economic scene. World War II further heightened and quickened these changes.

The economy at large had altered too; the machine had become an ever-increasing factor in human life. This was reflected in fashions. Cheap, machine-made cloths became available. Textile technology developed new synthetic fabrics, from which lingerie could be factory-made. Women of all classes could afford to buy cheap yet attractive clothes. The old necessity for women to know how to sew and repair their own clothes became less crucial.

People's living habits changed too. No longer did girls accumulate huge trousseaux of hand-made lingerie and household linen. With the disappearance of servant labour, living conditions became simpler, houses smaller. Elaborate table linen, requiring careful laundering, starching and ironing, was kept for very formal occasions only, or replaced altogether by lightweight

Traditional 17th-century designs on a sampler worked in 1931 by Joan Drew, who started the needlework collection now housed at Guildford Museum.

Embroidered panel designed by Edward Burne-Jones and William Morris *c*1870, worked in coloured wools on linen.

tablecloths or table mats and small napkins. Everywhere in the house, plastics and synthetics, which are cheap and easy to clean, took over.

As women studied more and took up more responsible jobs, their leisure time shrank and their need for labour-saving devices grew. Paper handkerchiefs and napkins came into use. Lightweight, non-iron bed linen became popular. This, like modern table linen, can be gaily coloured and printed, or machine-embroidered; it requires no further ornamentation. No one would think of regarding such goods as heirlooms and there is therefore no call for careful hand-marking with the owner's monogram.

Towards the end of the 19th century, embroidery had become debased. The decorative arts, generally, are at their best when they serve an essential, practical need; when work and utility are divorced, craftsmanship is liable to deteriorate. The Victorians ignored this principle and spent much time and effort working on specimens of no real value. William Morris scorned the useless fancy work which occupied the leisure hours of so many Victorian women. At an early stage, he had become interested in embroidery, and the patterns he designed and worked of birds and flowering trees contrasted

A canvas stitch sampler depicting a multitude of fabulous beasts including a mermaid, griffins, Pegasus, a unicorn, a centaur, the Sphinx and the Phoenix.

boldly with the fussy, garishly coloured, fashionable embroidery of the time. The crewel wools Morris used had been specially dyed for him in subtle shades. His wife and daughters worked with him. The former recalled how Morris himself had taught her 'the first principles of laying the stitches together so as to cover the ground smoothly and radiating them properly . . . we studied old pieces and by unpicking them, we learnt much—but it was uphill work . . . only carried through by his enormous energy and perseverance.' The novelist Henry James was struck by Morris's versatility, his apparent ability to turn his hand to anything from the manufacture of stained-glass windows to embroidering altar-cloths and designing wallpaper. Morris disliked the excessive realism of the pictorial embroidery which was then in fashion. In *Hints on Pattern Designing* he wrote, 'it is quite a delightful idea to cover a piece of linen with roses, jonquils and tulips done quite naturally with a needle and we cannot go too far in this direction, if only we remember the needs of our material and the nature of the craft in general.'

William Morris produced and sold the very first embroidery kits from his own firm, Morris, Marshall, Faulkner and Company, established in 1861. His idea was taken up by the Royal School of Needlework, founded in 1872 by Lady Marion Alford who shared Morris's horror of Berlin work, even if she sometimes found his flower and foliage patterns somewhat overwhelming. In 1886, writing in *Needlework as Art*, she compared Morris's favourite subjects to a 'kitchen garden in a tornado'. The Royal School of Needlework stressed from the very start the importance of studying and repairing old embroideries. Many old designs were copied and sold as patterns or as kits—activities which still go on at the School today.

In this century, Mrs Archibald Christie did much to instil new life into embroidery. She, like Morris, believed that 'it is a mistake in embroidery, as in all decorative arts to be realistic. . . .' She taught at the Royal College of Art in London, and in 1920 published a book entitled *Samplers and Stitches*,

Sampler worked in yellow-ochre mercerized cotton on linen using buttonhole, eye, single faggot, double faggot, four-sided, straight gobelin and satin stitches; wave stitch filling; drawn square and back stitches. The edges are finished with buttonhole stitch and ring-picots.
Helen Gowrie of Dunfermline, 1939. 21½ × 9½in.

Elizabethan blackwork designs worked in blue silk on linen. Marked SBS 1928.

which ran into several editions and is still compulsory reading for the professional or amateur needle-worker. In the introduction to her work, she wrote: 'Perfect expression is not attained by absolute imitation. . . . There is a place for nature and one for art, and when nature is adapted to artistic uses it needs a certain formalism to make it suit its artificial environment . . . flowers may be on the table in vases . . . laid on the table as decoration, but they must not be incorporated with the table linen . . . that is embroidered upon it, with any pretence that they are real flowers. . . .'

Today, one of the main values of embroidery is that it creates something individual. At a time when so many of the objects that surround us are mass-produced and stereotyped, a handmade or hand-ornamented article has an aura of quality that the machine is powerless to imitate. This does not mean, of course, that the machine is to be despised. Many modern embroiderers have used it to great advantage. For example, in Rene Dmytrenko's view of old Rochdale, done in machine embroidery and highlighted with hand stitches, the artist uses the machine as a tool, exploiting its possibilities to create new effects. Lillian Delevoryas is another modern embroiderer who has mastered the old techniques but uses and combines them in a completely new way. Her panel 'Seascape' is a notable example. Because it uses a variety of stitches, it can be called a modern sampler. Note the use of bargello to suggest the foliage of the tree; chain stitch, for the bottom shells on the left of the picture, creates an interesting relief effect over the Greek pattern of the border.

Such work demonstrates that the embroiderer's craft is still alive and has found new avenues of expression. During the first quarter of this century, much of the embroidery produced showed that, after the excesses of the 19th century, embroiderers wanted to go back to the past, copying pieces from the 17th and 18th centuries. Some valuable lessons were rediscovered and interesting work was produced. One example is the series of stall and chair cushions, and kneelers, that Louisa Pesel had completed by 1931 for the private chapel of the Bishop of Winchester at Wolvesey. Her designs were all adapted from 17th century samplers. She and her group of 200 workers later made another similar collection for Winchester Cathedral. Some embroiderers, however, did go too far in this cult of the past. They tried, for instance, to reproduce mellow colour harmonies that were largely the product of time alone. Mary Eirween Jones, in her *History of Western Embroidery*, wrote that, 'The workers forgot the dictum that the antique is good for inspiration but bad for slavish imitation.'

In the 1960s, art college students 'rediscovered' embroidery. Many of them scorned stitch discipline, wanting to create effects and textures with thread and needle in the way an abstract painter might use paint and brush. This was in direct opposition to what people like Mrs Christie had believed. 'Without stitches,' she wrote, 'there could be no art of embroidery. They are the means by which fanciful ideas and memories of pleasant things can be figured upon fabrics.' Happily, this principle has become accepted once again, as the modern samplers illustrated in this chapter indicate.

If young girls are no longer expected to produce two or more elaborate samplers at the end of their school careers, it does not mean that the sampler has disappeared from our life. Fashions are volatile, and what was once regarded as dated is now eagerly sought as Victoriana. This taste for the old

and the quaint has greatly helped in bringing about a revival of interest in samplers. Even the crowded, garishly coloured Victorian ones, so despised by experts like A. F. Kendrick, are now regarded as naive relics of the past, of a way of life gone forever. In many cases, their once strident hues have mellowed with age, lending them a new charm. Samplers are now collected and sold at ever-increasing prices.

The advertising and business world have been quick to realize the potentialities of samplers, and have used their association with tradition to promote all kinds of product: garden fertilizers, paints, home removals, a famous brand of tomato ketchup, a flower delivery service. Samplers have been reproduced on gift-wrapping paper, chocolate boxes, greeting cards and on countless other things. Some of the largest toy manufacturers have produced sampler kits for children; the government-sponsored Design Centre in London set its seal on some, and the National Trust of Great Britain has produced its own design for sale in stately homes. Queen Elizabeth II's Silver Jubilee was marked by the Royal School of Needlework's special sampler kit.

Embroidery kits do have their advantages. But it is also rather sad that

Left. Sampler in Hungarian flame stitch and knot stitch.
Right. 'Seascape'. Needlework picture by Lillian Delevoryas.

Opposite. This family record sampler, made by Edith Roosevelt, wife of American President Theodore Roosevelt in 1925, could be adapted to incorporate events from your own family life. The top row shows Mr and Mrs Roosevelt with their six children; row 2, their home and family pets; row 3, reading from left to right, positions held by Roosevelt from Commissioner of the Civil Service to the Vice Presidency; row 4, in the centre, the Washington Monument symbolises the peak of his career when he became President. Other motifs record his favourite pursuits as an explorer, hunter and writer. Row 5: patriotic emblems recalling World War I, with the San Quentin Star for the son killed and three soldiers for the sons that returned.

The Old Rochdale Market which no longer exists. This embroidered picture was designed and worked in 1975 by Rene Dmytrenko from her own photograph of the site. It is worked in a multiplicity of machine and hand stitches.

so many people feel that they must rely on someone else to create a design, choose a colour scheme and even cut the thread to required lengths, instead of creating something entirely their own. Winifred Clayton, who has practised and taught embroidery all her life, believes that anyone is capable of creating a design. As her series of three samplers demonstrates, it is possible, starting with a circular shape divided into three sections, to produce a design of a complexity that grows with the embroiderer's knowledge of stitches and her confidence. The third sampler includes several stitches, appliqué technique and beading, and its design could easily be developed further or repeated to produce an attractive piece of work.

Modern samplers used as teaching aids often take the form of the one described above—a small piece of fabric, carefully mounted on cardboard. A similar presentation in samplers, illustrated in this chapter, is by Heide Jenkins, an ex-student of the London College of Fashion. All are working samplers that explore the possibilities of a particular stitch or technique. For example, the three samplers made by Margaret Nicholson, a lecturer at the College, illustrate various kinds of pulled thread work, done in wool and on unexpected fabrics. A quite remarkable lacy effect is created by removing thread both ways in an already loosely woven fabric and joining the groups of thread with spiders embroidered in random-coloured mohair wool. Sheila Rose's sampler demonstrates a more conventional use of the same technique.

It is interesting to note that in our century the sampler seems to have acquired a dual function: some use it as a record of stitches; other embroiderers make more conventional samplers, meant to be framed as decorative objects. Many samplers are made as gifts for someone, such as the one made

Blackwork sampler by Heide Jenkins, made as an Embroiderer's Guild examination piece. The right hand section shows the traditional use of blackwork contrasted with a freer modern interpretation on the left.

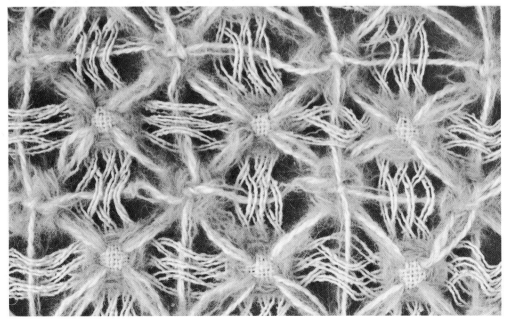

Drawn thread sampler. Mohair on loosely woven fabric. Threads have been pulled on both sides as on Sheila Rose's sampler. Margaret Nicholson.

126

Drawn thread work in an unusual medium: wool on hessian. Worked by Margaret Nicholson as a teaching aid for the London College of Fashion.

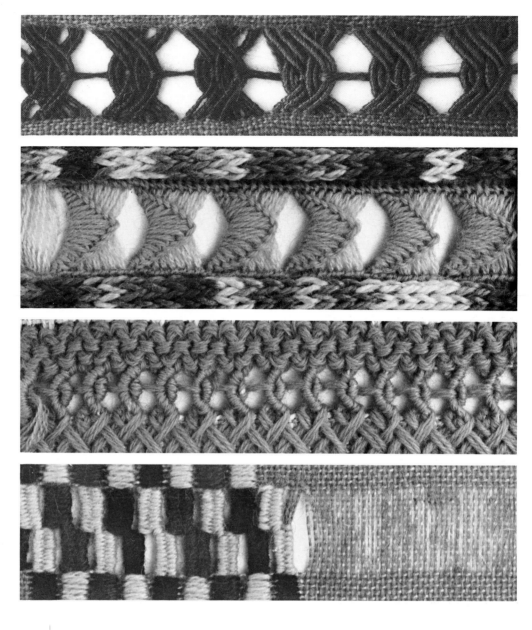

Overleaf. Sections of a book sampler worked on Binca cloth by Winifred Clayton. This was done to show the potentialities of a medium often used in schools, though not always in an interesting fashion. The colour plate on the right is the last page of the book.

Similar drawn thread work in a more conventional style by Sheila Rose.

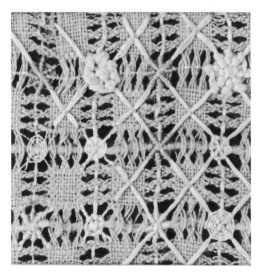

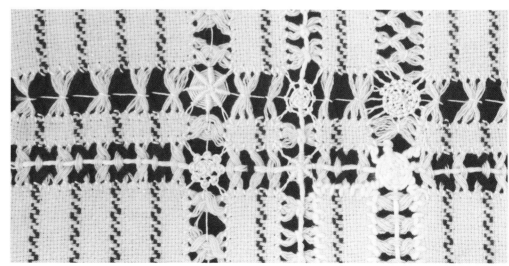

by Edith Roosevelt in 1925, which depicts momentous events in Theodore Roosevelt's life. More recent is a genealogical sampler recording the dates and provenance of the earliest American samplers. A charming example is a piece dated 1972, which bemoans the fate of the London market area of Covent Garden, which was under the threat of demolition.

Earlier in this century, few people made samplers except for the apprentices of the City and Guilds of London Institute, the Royal School of Needlework and other colleges. Their work tended to be quite simple, showing the

Above. The tale of Pollock's Toy Museum and its move from Soho to Scala Street in 1972 on a sampler worked by Deborah Brown.

Left. This silk embroidered picture on damask, based on an illustration by William Blake, shows the increasing level of sophistication which can be found in 20th-century embroidery.

Embroiderers' Guild examination piece worked in 1935.

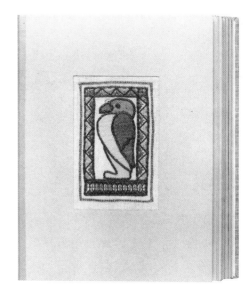

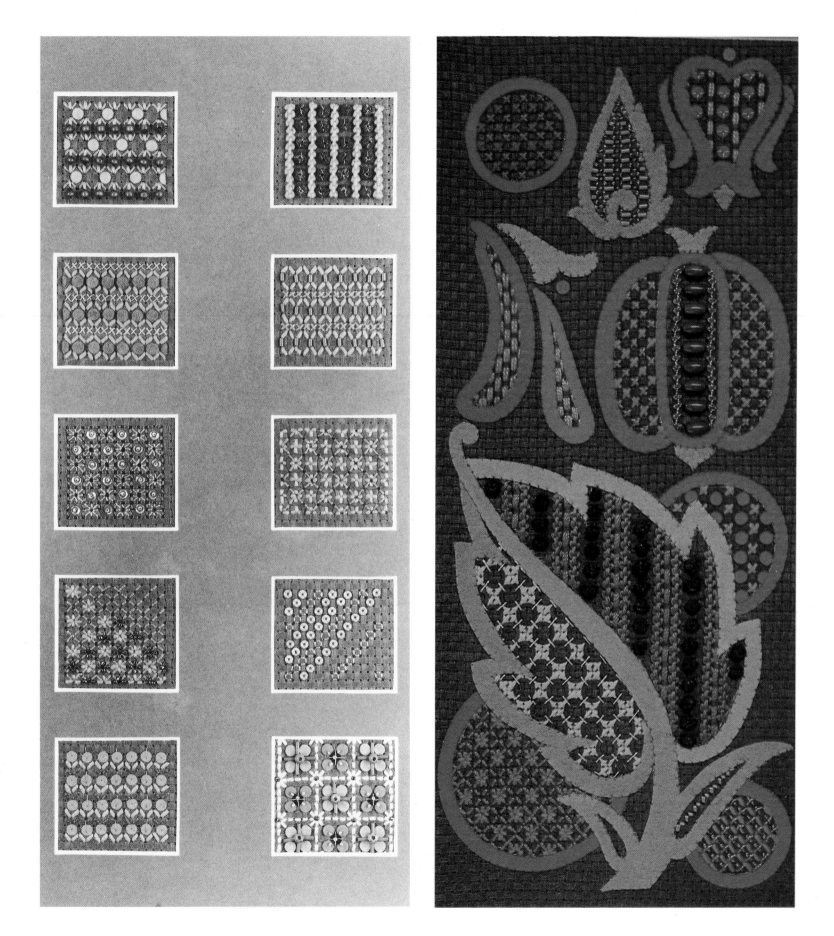

129

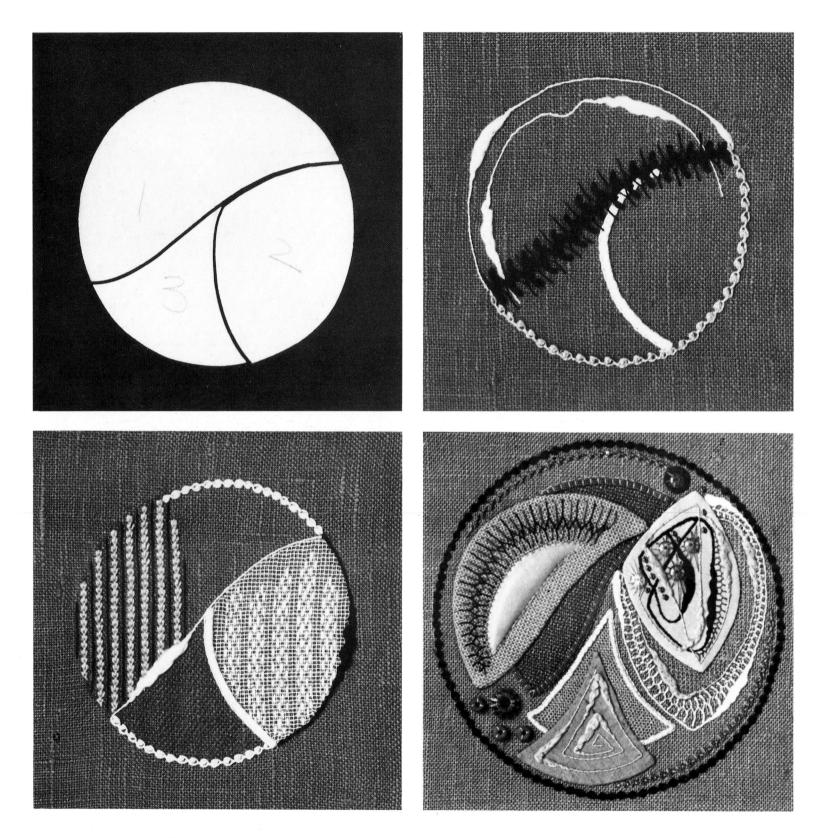

Above. A sampler worked by Winifred Clayton which shows how the same basic design can be used to produce a more complex pattern as the embroiderer's skill and confidence grows.

A traditional sampler made by Deborah Brown's mother in 1938.

Below. This sampler picture, in four panels, celebrates the Coronation of King George V in 1911.

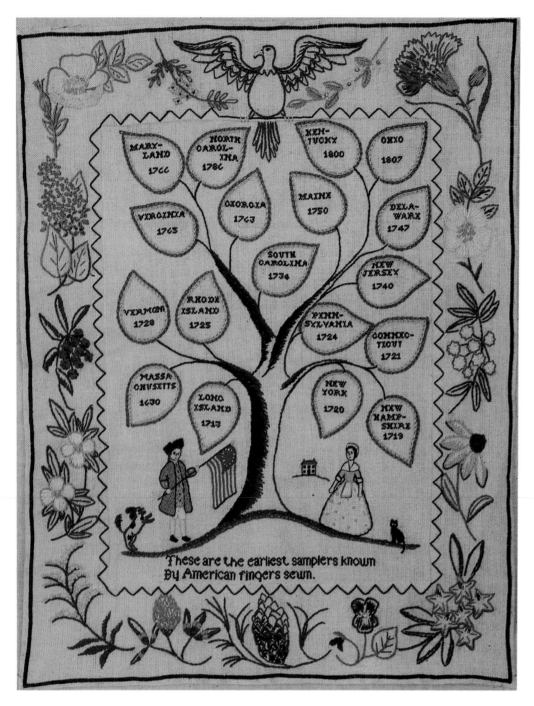

The sampler shows a tree with leaves bearing the names and dates:

MARY-LAND 1766, NORTH CAROL-INA 1786, KEN-TUCKY 1800, OHIO 1807, OXOROXA 1743, MAINE 1750, VIRGINIA 1765, DELA-WARE 1747, SOUTH CAROLINA 1734, NEW JERSEY 1740, VERMONT 1728, RHODE ISLAND 1725, PENN-SYLVANIA 1724, CONNEC-TICUT 1721, MASSA-CHUSETTS 1630, LONG ISLAND 1713, NEW YORK 1720, NEW HAMP-SHIRE 1719

*These are the earliest samplers known
By American fingers sewn.*

Left. This contemporary sampler by Josephine Boyle gives the dates of the earliest known samplers found in the American Colonies. The flowers round the border are the floral emblems of the different states.

The two pictures below demonstrate how the sampler can be used as a potent commercial gimmick – either as a packaging idea for Whitman 'Sampler' chocolates or as advertising for Pickford's Removals.

Whitman's Sampler. CHOCOLATES & CONFECTIONS. NET WT. 16 OZ. (1 LB.) 453 GRAMS

HOME MOVING GUIDE. Pickfords

use of various stitches; alternatively they were sewing samplers, displaying dress-making and mending processes. Such work was a relic from the late 19th century charity schools, and it continued until the early 1930s. In schools, simple samplers, showing alphabets, numerals and a basic design, were also still being made.

The present revival of interest in samplers is not confined to Britain. In America, in Germany and elsewhere, people are rediscovering them. They enjoy recording family and public events in stitches. There is no limit to the subject range, whether one chooses to copy an old specimen or to devise a new one. Anything that can be translated into simple shapes is suitable: house or garden, pets, simple landscapes and maps, plants and flowers, and

This delightful large sampler is used as a screen by the maker. It is another example of the family record sampler showing the New York and country homes of the family, the French father and American mother with their three sons and family dogs, assorted pets and the family's love for the sea around Martha's Vineyard.

verses. The style can be traditional or modern. Even working from a kit can be a pleasant experience. Many people who have since become very interested in original embroidery, started out with a printed pattern or a ready-to-sew kit that had caught their eye.

Some needlework teachers in adult education centres refuse to let students work from kits, believing that people must first acquire a proper grounding before they can be allowed to go on with a piece of work. Others are quite happy to let them work on a bought kit, in the hope that the students may develop a deeper interest, practise and increase their repertoire of stitches, just as one would build up a vocabulary in a foreign language. With a good command of stitches—and that means not merely being able to produce a stitch but knowing the effect it will have on different fabrics, done in different sizes with different types of threads—it becomes possible for the embroiderer to produce designs, not necessarily very elaborate or time-consuming but possessing true originality and character. Modern embroiderers think that good design can be ruined by the wrong choice of stitch. Schools of embroidery today make deliberate efforts to bring together the creative artist and the technical worker so that a designer, even if not a practical embroiderer, may create designs suitable for the craft. The Needlework Development Scheme, founded in 1934 to encourage greater interest in embroidery and to raise the standard of design, was a pioneer in this area. Over the years, it built up an impressive collection of British and foreign embroidered pieces, both traditional and modern. The collection was packed in boxes which were available on loan to art schools, training colleges, women's institutes and schools. The Scheme's publications, *And So To Sew* and *And So To Embroider*, were released to schools and were instrumental in the revival of interest in needlework at school levels. Whereas many adult women have rather nasty memories of the weekly ordeal in the needlework class, today's children—boys included—appear to enjoy this activity and often produce quite stunning pieces of work. The Needlework Development Scheme was closed in 1961 because it was felt that it had fulfilled its fundamental aims. The collection, which by then included over 3,500 embroideries, was given to various establishments. The most important pieces were donated to the Victoria and Albert Museum in London and to the Royal Scottish Museum in Edinburgh.

We live in an age when the pace of life has become very rapid and people often find it difficult to unwind at the end of the day. Needlework addicts will testify to the therapeutic effects of an evening spent embroidering. Some people are deterred by the idea that embroidery requires a super-human amount of patience. True, working a series of twelve covers for a set of dining room chairs or a reticella tablecloth will be a lengthy process. But an attractive piece of work can easily be produced in a few days or weeks. What better way to start than with a sampler?

At the end of this section the reader will find a modern sampler design that was created specially for this book. The sampler is accompanied by a sketch which the reader can reproduce or use as a starting point for designing and working her own sampler. A complete list of the stitches used is given, but this is purely a guide and the same design, worked in different stitches and in another colour scheme, would look equally good and yet entirely different. The secret behind the charm of old samplers was their individuality, their personal character. This is just about the only principle anyone wishing to start a sampler should remember.

Danish pulled thread sampler worked by Winifred Clayton.

PRACTICAL - 20th CENTURY

WORKING SAMPLER EXPERIMENTS

Embroidery is more than just surface ornament. In many ways it is like reweaving the cloth, modifying it with more versatility than a loom could achieve, and a whole variety of different effects can be produced on a single piece of fabric. Textures with pulled or drawn threads, lace and mesh brocades, pattern-woven darns, honeycomb and raised work are a few of the effects available to the embroiderer.

There are only two really important technical points to remember. First, the background fabric, if it is not to be entirely covered, is not simply an anchor for thread. The stitches should appear to be part of it, so that when they are completed they will together with the fabric form a piece of textile. It matters a good deal to the embroidery whether the background is rough or smooth and whether it is a brilliant bleached white, or more yellow or brown, or an adventurous bright colour.

Second, consider the natural properties of the stitches and use these to achieve effects. Do not, for instance, force cross stitches into elaborate curves; exploit their stepped, zig-zag quality.

Experiment. Spread stitches out, or pack them closer together, elongate or shorten strokes, pull them tighter or looser than usual, or bunch them together in double or treble groups. The best effect may be on the reverse side.

Fillings made with stitches not normally used for the purpose can also produce interesting results. A buttonhole or stem stitch worked in alternate directions, for example, may make a ribbed or plaited surface.

Patterns can also be worked in reverse, so that it is the background which is worked, leaving the design as bare fabric. This 'voiding', when worked in cross or square stitches, is sometimes called Assisi work and is found a good deal in Italian embroidery. Italian samplers of the 17th century often show it, but it is less common in English work.

It is a good idea to make a collection of experimental yarns, in addition to those specially produced for embroidery. Generally, threads which pierce the fabric, unless it is a canvas mesh, need to be smooth. But such things as knotted string or slubbed wools can be couched down.

At Christmas in particular, all kinds of interesting, fancy parcel twines are available. Some plaited tinsel braids can be couched and interlaced and are very much like the 17th-century embroidered braids. One note of caution: these may not be washable. Invisible mending threads on a loose mesh net curtaining can make a very delicate spider's web fabric. Modern synthetic fabrics frequently have properties which can be played around with before embroidery starts. Pleating and folding can often be fixed with the heat of an iron. Holes that do not actually need to be sewn to prevent them from fraying can be made with a hot skewer or similar instrument. On the whole the heavier weight fabrics are easiest to sew. And the less slippery they are, the better.

Fur or pile fabrics, apart from velvet, have been entirely overlooked. A small comb is useful to divide the pile into partings, some of which can be couched down, leaving sections standing or protruding through rows of embroidery stitches. Stretch fabrics can be pulled and gathered or have slots cut on the bias. Portions can be laddered, making a good basis for needleweaving or a variety of hem-stitches.

Sequins and spangles need a little care. They lose their effect when piled on like crown jewels. Try mixing them with dull threads or knotted or textured stitches. 'Beads' can also be found among electrical component parts: china insulators, washers and colourful transistors from radios. Printed circuits may give ideas for labyrinthine patterns.

A sampler notebook is a very useful thing. When visiting museums, take a small pocketbook (with a stiff piece of cardboard in it to rest on), a firm dark pencil, three coloured pencils and an eraser. Four pencils are usually enough to distinguish between parts of patterns. Samplers on general display are seldom at the right height, not near enough to see clearly or without a light beaming on the glass. Aim for the general shape and feel of the embroidery in your drawing, and if you can get close enough, count stitches up and across the motif at the essential points. From this, you can work out the details later. Notes on colour can be written down. Sampler traditions are thus carried on, with motifs borrowed from mothers' or grandmothers' samplers, but not copied stitch for stitch. A notebook is also useful for jotting and scribbling things to be used when making your own designs. Walks in town or country alike will provide a mass of ideas. Things to look for might include colour combinations that are unusual or appeal to you; for example, wet brick walls may be yellow, red-pink, purple-grey, green with damp or lichen, or full of holes like a sponge cake.

Embroideries inspired by natural objects need to have some of the features of the thing, whether naturalistically drawn or in a more abstract pattern. So make notes on the way tree branches spring from the trunk, the directions of growth in bushes, the characteristic shapes of plants. Illustrations of plants in catalogues and on seed packets are quite useful, as it is their purpose to show flowers, fruit, leaves and roots clearly – just as Elizabethan embroiderers used drawing of 'slips' or cuttings from gardening books and herbals.

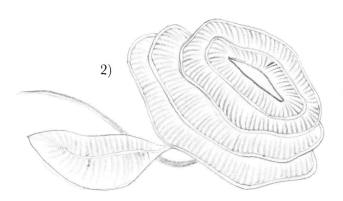

These sketches suggest how similar motifs can be worked in different ways.

1) Darned motifs with stem stitch outlines. The darns are mainly plain and twills.
   Stripes are used purely for decoration, and are not intended to imitate a naturalistic pattern of light and shade.

2) Flower worked in rings of buttonhole stitch.

3) Motifs worked in satin and stem stitches. The stylized tree is worked in radiating long and short satin stitches, with stem stitch worked in ribs along the trunk.

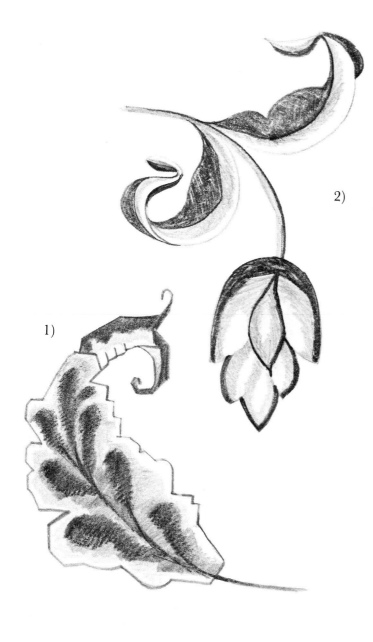

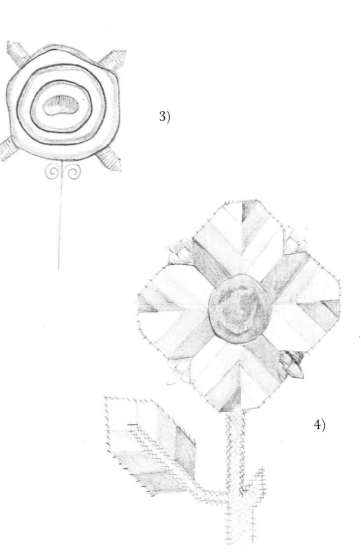

1) Tent stitch leaf showing naturalistic curl but formalized by the necessary squareness of stitch.

2) Satin stitch flower showing a similar curving treatment and use of contrasting colours.

3) Rose 'slip' made from concentric circles of detached buttonhole or lace stitch, shaded dark towards the outer edge. Satin stitch centre and leaves and double running stem.

4) Formalized 'slip' rose outlined in long armed cross stitch with flower and leaves worked detached, in lace stitches, which are applied to the background and couched down around the edges. The centre is worked a little too large, to give it a puffed, three-dimensional effect.

5) Formalized honeysuckle flower worked in leaf, satin and long armed cross stitches with double running tendrils.

A WORKING SAMPLER

1) A long linen or cotton strip is still one of the most practical forms for a working sampler. As it has no defined border, stitches can go on being added or further pieces of fabric attached as necessary. A long strip, made up from several sorts of linens and canvases, provides space for a great variety of stitches and experiments. A mixture of loose and closely woven fabrics should be chosen, and also dark and light colours. For neatness, the pieces can be joined with fagotting, or oversewn edge-to-edge; to be kept in the workbox, they can be rolled up on a piece of dowelling, or on a wooden knitting needle passed through the top hem.

2) Alternatively, a sampler that will fold flat accordion fashion can be made with several pieces of fabric bound with ribbon or bias binding.

3) A separate case or cover can be made to keep the sampler clean.

4) A sampler can also take the form of a book. For this, covers should be stiffened with card, but there should be a broad soft spine with about ten tucks sewn down its length so that they project inwards.
The bound 'pages' of embroidery can then be sewn in—one to each tuck. This is an attractive way of making a finished sampler as a present.

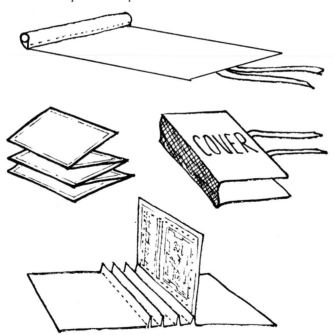

Do not line the back of a working sampler, as the reverse will explain how the stitches were worked.

The name of the stitch and working instructions can be added quite neatly by sewing a strip of white tape or paper underneath the rows of embroidery.

STITCH CATEGORIES

A careful look at various embroidery stitches quickly reveals that however complicated they may appear, they can be grouped under about six main families of stitches. Once the basic stitch is mastered, it is relatively easy to learn its many variations. For instance, double feathering is basically a buttonhole stitch arranged in a zig-zag pattern. This book does not attempt to demonstrate every possible stitch, but concentrates on those which appeared on samplers at various periods. The bibliography mentions several reference books which will give working instructions for any stitch not included in this book. The list below lists the stitches shown in this book under their various categories:

Stroke Stitches

Satin	Split
Cushion	Tent
Long and short	Gobelin
Stem	Eye
Crewel	Algerian eye
Back	Florentine
Running	Hungarian
Double running or Holbein	

Buttonhole Stitches

Buttonhole	Feather
Hollie point	Ladder
Buttonhole wheels and eyelets	Roman
Oriental or Roumanian	

Cross

Cross	Herringbone
17th-century cross	Fishbone or Spanish plait
2-sided Italian cross	Cretan
Long armed cross	Rococo
Montenegrin cross	Berlin cross stitches
Roumanian cross	
Square or single faggot	

Chain

Chain
Open chain
Coral or snail trail
Wheat-ear

Knot Stitches

French knots
Bullion bars

Overcast Stitches

Overcast
Russian overcast
Russian drawn
Needleweaving
Couching

TRANSFERRING DESIGNS

Pricking using chalk and charcoal

For this method, the design should ideally be on tracing paper, so that it can be placed accurately on the fabric.

With a medium-fine needle, prick the outline through the paper from the wrong side, keeping the holes even and close together. A fold of paper or a cork on the end of the needle will make it easier to hold.

Place the pricked pattern on the fabric and with drawing pins fasten both layers to a drawing board or a wooden tea tray.

If transferring to a dark fabric, use ground pumice or, if this is not available, chalk; if the fabric is light-coloured, use drawing charcoal. (Both these are easily crushed in a paper bag with a hammer or rolling pin.)

Make a firm pad by rolling a strip of felt, and dip it into the powder. Rub it firmly over the perforated area. Tip out the excess powder back into its container.

This method is not permanent. After the pattern has been removed, the lines must be painted on with a fine brush (sable) and water colour paint (white on a dark fabric, light red on a light one). If the fabric has a fluffy surface (like felt), put a little domestic soap on the brush. This will make the paint adhere to the fabric. The transfer is now a stencil and can be reused.

Stencils

All sorts of stencil can easily be made from stiff paper, using a craft tool knife. For drawing out repeat patterns, stencils are invaluable, as they can be reversed by turning them over and made to turn corners accurately by working off a 45° line.

To make stencils from leaves, as an alternative to drawing them, first choose a well-shaped example. Pick it when it is green and place it between two sheets of writing paper or thin cartridge paper. Press with a hot iron on a firm surface for several minutes. The impression will then be left on the paper, which can be cut out. To stiffen the stencil, varnish it.

Transfers

Ready-printed transfers for embroidery can be bought from haberdashery departments of stores, but they are usually very dull. Special blue pencils can also be bought, and you can use these to make your own transfers. (They can be obtained from the manufacturers: Messrs Lowe & Carr, Eastern Boulevard, Leicester). Tissue paper is best to work on, as it allows you to see through to the fabric beneath and place the pattern accurately. Do not use tracing paper: this burns under the iron.

1) Draw your pattern on a piece of good drawing paper. Place the tissue over it, pin it down and trace over the design with the blue pencil. Keep the pencil sharp, as the lines should not be thick.

2) To trace a design from an existing piece of embroidery or from a delicate book, place a sheet of transparent plastic or glass over the work. Put a sheet of tracing paper on top and secure it with sticky tape to the glass (and not the embroidery). Trace the design with a pencil. To transfer the design so that it comes out the same way round as the original, turn the tracing paper over, put a sheet of tissue on top and trace again with the blue pencil. The design may now be ironed off. In ironing transfers, it is important not to rub backwards and forwards as in normal ironing; press straight down, lift the iron off and move to the next area to avoid smudging. Transfers will usually work a second time although they will be rather paler. However, the lines can be gone over again with the pencil.

Carbon Paper

Special dressmaker carbon paper—not the office type—should be used. It usually comes in packets containing several colours—blue, white and yellow or orange—so that it will show up on different coloured fabrics.

Place the fabric on a wooden board, put the carbon paper face-downwards on top of it, and the design on top of that. Pin the whole sandwich to the board. (Pins should not go through the carbon paper as they will make a mark, so if necessary cut the carbon to the size of the design.)

Pressing evenly, go over the outlines with a hard pencil, an empty ball point pen or a small knitting needle. The resulting impression should be faint. Care is needed to avoid smudges and unwanted marks.

Rubbings

This method should not be used on old or fragile embroideries, as it will tend to flatten the embroidery. The special impression paper and wax used for taking brass rubbings will give the best results; provided the paper used is thin and strong (air-mail paper is quite adequate), a sufficiently clear image will result.

Place the paper over the embroidery and tape to the table or board beneath. Using a thick wax crayon, rub over the surface, working in one direction only. This is a quick method, but not precise; the blurred edges will need to be drawn in afterwards, as well as any low relief details.

Enlarging and Reducing

To avoid spoiling the original drawing, a tracing should be made. Enclose the design within a rectangle, and divide it into numbered squares.

To enlarge, extend the bottom line to the required length. With a set square, draw a new side line at right angles to the first. Then take a diagonal line from the bottom left corner until it crosses the new right side line. This will tell you the height of the enlarged rectangle.

Re-draw this new rectangle size on another sheet of paper. Divide this into the same number of numbered squares as on the original (the squares will now be larger) and re-draw the design square by square.

To reduce: begin by making the base line shorter then proceed in the same way.

NEEDLE AND THREAD

Generally, yarns that are soft and only slightly twisted will best fit a flat eyed needle. Those with a firm twist are round in section and need a round or 'egg eyed' needle. The purpose of choosing the right size is to make a hole in the fabric just large enough for the yarn to pass through without roughening it. If the hole made is too small, it will be hard work pushing the needle through and will spoil the thread. If the hole is too large, it will show on the finished work. This is an advantage in pulled thread work, but on a close grained fabric it looks poor and prevents the placing of stitches accurately or close together.

A needle for each job

Crewel needles, as their name suggests, are for that sort of woollen embroidery worked on linen with a variety of free embroidery stitches that do not rely on counting threads. They have a very sharp point and a long flat eye, ideal for sewing with soft, slightly twisted wools, cottons or stranded embroidery cottons.

Tapestry needles have a large eye and a rounded blunt point, designed for canvas and counted thread embroidery in which it is important to separate the threads of the fabric without splitting them. These are also useful for sewing other fabrics to heavyweight linen.

Sharps are the workaday plain sewing needles. They are shorter in general than the other sorts, sharp-pointed and with rounded eyes. These are good for fine work with a twisted thread.

For free designs in thick threads, use chenille needles. These are sharp, and have large eyes to take the fluffy, round, chenille threads.

Variety packets of needles will give a selection of these, with the exception of chenilles. Get a good selection and do not try to sew with the same needle for everything. An emery bag is very useful for polishing needles and will prevent rust and stickiness. It will also help to keep them sharp. Synthetic fabrics in particular will blunt needles quite quickly.

All beginners, children in particular, often find it difficult and frustrating to keep on threading needles and this frequently puts them off sewing altogether. To start with it is hard to manipulate the needle and keep the thread anchored in it at the same time. Threading can be facilitated in several ways. First, it is important to have a good, cleanly cut end of thread to work with. Apart from various sorts of wire threaders, cotton yarns can be stiffened at the end by drawing them through a beeswax block or a piece of dry soap. It is easier to thread wool if the end is doubled over before insertion through the eye of the needle.

Once threaded, the yarn can be anchored in the needle by putting the point of the needle through the short end of the thread; this will make a split stitch loop which will hold firm.

The term 'bodkin' is nowadays confusingly applied to both the sharp instrument used for making holes in cloth and to the large-eyed, blunt needle made for threading elastic. The latter is very useful for sewing open-meshed fabrics.

EMBROIDERY FRAMES

Embroidery frames come in two basic types – the circular tambour frame and the rectangular slate frame. The purpose of an embroidery frame is to stretch the fabric taut, ensuring that warp and weft threads remain square, enabling the embroiderer to produce accurate, even stitchery. This is particularly important for stroke stitches such as satin stitch or couching where the thread needs to lie flat on the surface. When a stitch is worked by going in and out of the fabric in the same movement, as in feather or chain stitch, a frame is unsuitable.

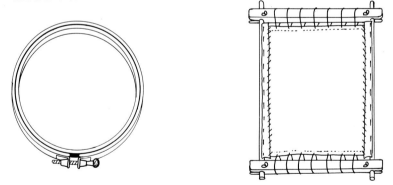

Tambour frames consist of two wooden (or occasionally metal) rings. The fabric is put over the inner ring, and the outer one is placed on top of it and tightened with a screw. To prevent marking areas already worked, and to ensure a good grip on slippery material it is advisable to bind the inner ring with broad bias tape.

Setting up a slate frame is known as dressing the frame. It consists of two stretchers or side pieces and two rollers with webbing nailed to them. These frames are adjustable and are usually tightened with pegs or wing nuts. The width of the fabric to be embroidered should not be larger than the width of the webbing on the rollers, but the length does not matter as the excess is wound round the rollers and moved up as required. Make a 1.5 cm turning at the top and bottom of the fabric, and sew tape along the sides. Mark the centre of the webbing and fold the fabric to find the middle. Hem the top and bottom of the fabric to the webbing. Assemble the frame, winding any extra fabric around the bottom roller, and tighten the pegs or nuts. Next, lace the sides of the fabric to the stretchers, through the tape, using thin string or cord. Lace one side first and wind string around some part of the frame. Then lace the other side and adjust the tension before fastening the string.

BEGINNING AND FINISHING A PIECE OF EMBROIDERY

To start, run a few stitches (to be worked over) on the right side of the fabric. Alternatively, begin with a half stitch of whichever sort is being used. For proper sewing, knots should never be used. They are lumpy and can easily come undone. The exception to this is when it is necessary, perhaps on a working sampler, to show exactly where the beginning is. It is sometimes helpful to emphasise this by threading on a little bead.

In finishing, threads should be run in at the back of the work and spare ends cut off immediately. Loose threads at the back will tangle and get sewn into new work, making a mess.

If mistakes happen, it is usually best to cut through the stitches with a pair of sharp-pointed scissors, remove the bits of thread with tweezers. Unpicking will loosen the fabric, pull other stitches and often leave a coloured fuzz where the stitches have been, and, in any case, the saved thread is generally too scruffy to be reused.

Thread of all sorts should be cut, not broken. Breaking weakens thread considerably. Breaking also makes it difficult to thread the needle and, if fastening off, breaking will pull completed work.

THE SAMPLER PATTERN

The sampler on p. 142 was designed and worked specially for this book. Diagrams are included so that the pattern can be reproduced by those wishing to start a sampler without the trouble of devising their own. The patterns given throughout this book can also be combined to make a sampler. Do not be afraid to use elements of your everyday life: house, pets. Making a sampler is also a good opportunity to try out techniques and stitches you may not be familiar with. On a sampler it is possible to experiment with a small amount of a time-consuming technique such as reticella and discover that it may not be as difficult as it appears.

Before buying the cloth for your sampler, you should decide what type of embroidery you intend doing. A very fine Irish linen with 45 to 50 threads to the inch (2.5 cm) will be perfect for fine work, but remember that stitches will be very small and that any type of counted thread work (cross stitch, double running, etc.) will not only be more difficult to execute but that a fairly large area in this type of work will take a long time to embroider. In any case choose a soft, evenly woven cotton, wool or linen—29 threads to the inch is a good average—but a larger mesh (with fewer threads per inch) may be used if the sampler is to be worked in stranded wools rather than in stranded cottons. Select linen in its natural cream colour rather than bleached white. But coloured linen—yellow, pale green or brown—can look equally lovely. American samplers often owe their beauty and individuality to the bold contrast between the dark background cloth and the glowing colours of the embroidery.

When choosing embroidery threads, go to a well stocked shop and look at as large a selection as possible. Try the skeins against the cloth and one another. Good shops will usually exchange any unused skeins for others should the colours not work as well with one another as anticipated. Decide on a colour scheme and buy several shades of each colour rather than using too many different colours, as the design may lose coherence.

Our sampler design is quite large (56 × 40 cm) and will, of course, take a considerable time to work, particularly on a fine linen, as was used in this case. But you can make it smaller provided you keep the same proportions by reducing the pattern.

If you decide to work out your own design, plan the most important areas first—the border, a centre motif. Certain sections of the sampler can be emphasized in various ways: by using stronger colours, larger scale, thicker threads, etc. This will give visual interest and help to form the shape of the piece. Look at 18th century American samplers, in which the rectangular shape is very imaginatively divided up. You may decide to design the whole sampler on squared paper. Start by drawing your various motifs on separate pieces of paper and move them on the squared paper to see how they fit with one another. After finalizing the complete pattern on squared paper, transfer it on the cloth using one the methods recommended in this book.

For a more spontaneous result and perhaps more in keeping with the traditional concept of the sampler, you could choose to work out the areas like the border where corner areas will have to fit the size of the sampler on graph paper and trace or draw the remainder of the design freehand as you embroider.

Sampler instructions

Cut the fabric to size, allowing 5 cm all round for fraying and for a turnover or hem when the work is finished. If the fabric tends to fray a lot, do a row of machine stitching around the edge.

In our sampler we used the following colours:
Clark's Anchor stranded cotton: black (0403), pink (028).
Coats's Anchor stranded cotton: orange (0326), red (019), dark brown (0359), light brown (0355), beige (0372), grey (0392)

We used two strands unless otherwise stated. Use a tapestry needle.

Mark the dimensions of the pattern on the cloth with a pencil and find the centre either by folding or counting threads, transfer the diagrams on to the cloth.

Begin by embroidering the parts of the pattern to be worked in an embroidery frame, that is counted thread work—in this case the industrial landscape at the centre of the picture. This was done in black in a mixture of double running, stem and couched stitches. Still keeping the sampler in the frame, work the edging round the landscape. The inner and outer lines are worked in dark brown stem stitch. The arcaded pattern is four rows of chain stitch, worked close together in grey, beige, yellow and orange, which creates a shading. Fill in with bullion rolls, using the dark brown cotton.

Work the smaller diamond underneath, using the frame. Cast stitches along the whole length of one side of the diamond, using four strands of orange, aligning them neatly until the border is filled. Couch these threads criss-cross fashion with yellow cotton. Finish off the border with one row of brown stem stitch. Leave the lettering until your sampler is completed.

The electricity pylon border is worked in black, in stem stitch, the cables in double running stitch; the insulators are bullion rolls. Leave these until the end as you will need to remove the work from the frame to do them.

The brown outer edge of the border consists of a closely worked row of herringbone stitch, couched in grey in the middle. The inner and outer lines are in whipped running stitch, worked in beige and yellow.

Fill in the sampler, starting at the top with four rows of drawn thread work. The third row shows woven bars; the fourth is a pattern formed by combining woven and overcast bars. The section on reticella explains how to do these.

The next band consists of columns of buttonhole stitch worked closely together in red, pink, orange, pale brown and grey.

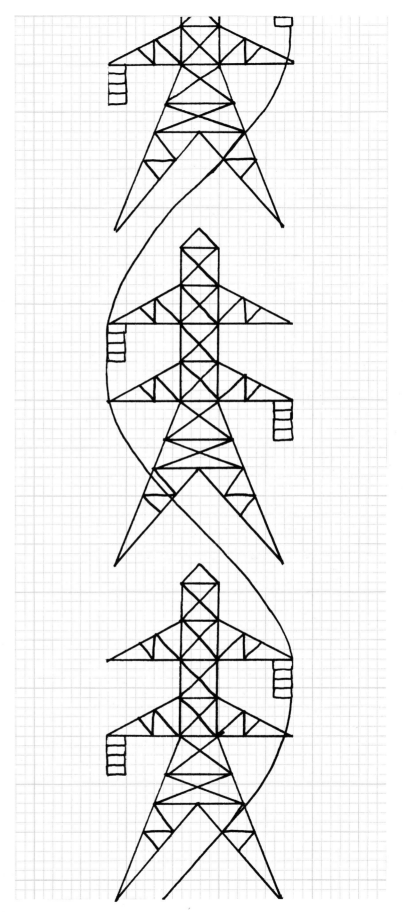

These are interspersed with squares of reticella worked in pale brown. This type of work is at its best in white—colour was selected for photographic reasons.

The spray of blossoms on the left was drawn freehand and worked in satin stitch. The petals can be made to look as if they are in different shades by varying the edge from which the stitches are worked. Work two French knots in yellow at the centre of each flower. The stems are stem stitch, using grey thread.

Work the foxgloves in long and short stitch, carefully radiating the stitches downward as the diagram shows. We used the red cotton with a touch of pink for the inside of the corolla. Finish off the outer edge of the corolla with one row of tiny stem stitches. This will add definition. Work the stamens by casting long stitches in beige and adding French knots at the end.

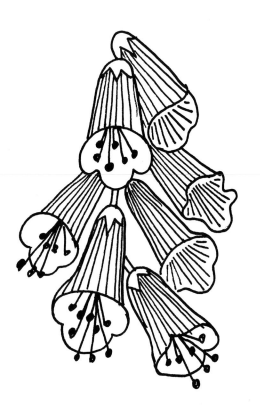

The maze on the bottom left is worked in stem, back, chain, heather and wheat-ear stitches. The red rosettes are in buttonhole stitch.

The maze on the other side is a mixture of stem and herringbone stitches. Work the wavy lines in couched stitch, using six strands and couching them with a contrasting colour. The rosettes are worked in herringbone stitch and the round spots in stem stitch. Start at the middle for these and work concentrically, keeping the lines of stitches close together.

Work the dog in long and short stitch, following the natural lines of the body. A mottled effect is achieved by using one strand of dark and one of light brown together. Patches on the back, the ear and the feet are worked in dark brown only. The belly area is worked by mixing light brown and beige.

Work the cat in stem stitch.

The yellow wavy lines isolating dog and cat are in coral stitch. Use three strands of cotton.

Last of all work the date, your name or initials. You will find alphabets and numerals on the endpapers of this book.

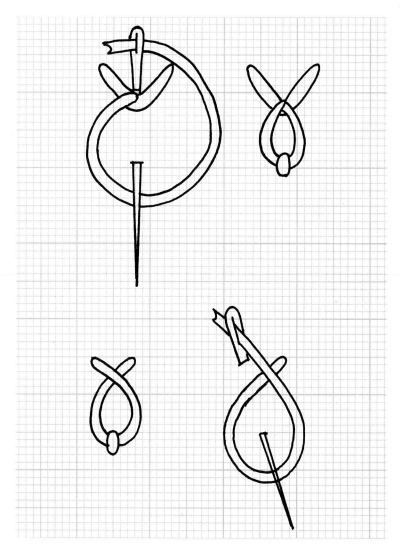

Wheat-ear stitch, also called *tête de boeuf*, a chain stitch which may be used singly or worked in continuous lines.

Crossed chain stitch. Variation of wheat-ear stitch.

Modern sampler, designed and worked by Deborah Brown and Mrinalini Srivastava.

Appendix 1 EUROPEAN & OTHER SAMPLERS

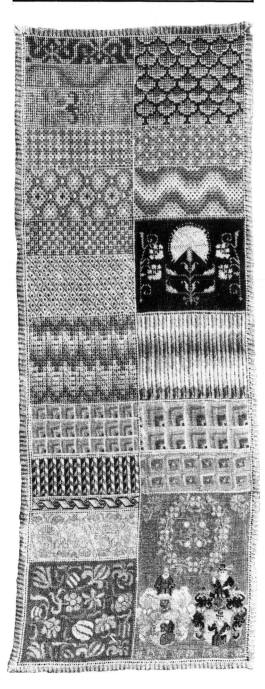

The early publication of pattern books in 16th century Germany shows that embroidery was widely practised and valued there. It is therefore little surprise that, after Britain, Germany appears to be the most prolific source of samplers. Although there is evidence that samplers were already worked in the 16th and 17th centuries, dated examples first seem to appear in the 18th century. One of the earliest, in the possession of the German Folklore Museum in Berlin, is a sampler dated 1704 and made in Döbeln, Saxony. It consists of six different border patterns, two alphabets and a series of numerals, followed by small random motifs—birds, flowers, small animals, crowns. Towards the bottom, a small cartouche contains initials and the date. The whole work is done in cross-stitch. It is a characteristic of German samplers that the stitch selection is far more limited than in English ones. This particular sampler retains the long shape associated with 17th century examples, but samplers gradually became square or, quite frequently, rectangular. The collection at Berlin includes some remarkable darning samplers which seem to have been more popular than they were in Britain. There are also many examples showing how to patch up worn linen, in which pieces of various shapes have been skilfully inserted. In the 19th century, samplers showing how to insert slits in men's shirts were popular school exercises. The top of the slit is carefully finished off in needlepoint lace.

Early German samplers were embroidered with linen or silk thread on unbleached linen. During the Biedermeier period—the early 19th century—as in Britain, tammy came in fashion. It was woven in narrow widths,

Right. German sampler from Vierlande, a district on the Elbe, near Hamburg, 1838. Worked in silk on linen in cross stitch, the alphabets, numerals, crowns and coronets are similar to those found on English and American samplers and were practised for the marking of precious household linen.

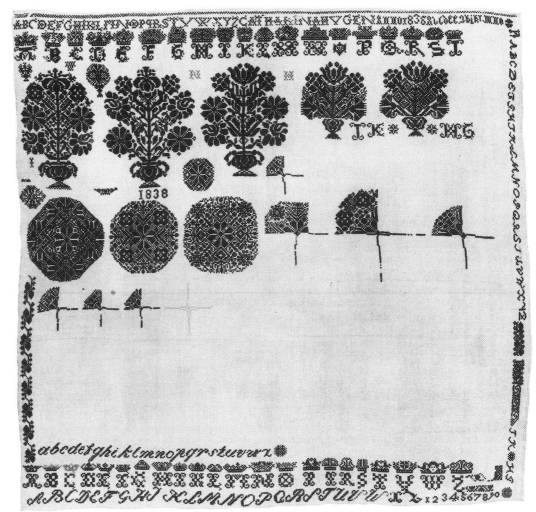

Opposite, left. South German sampler dated 1688. Coloured silk on linen canvas. Worked in tent, satin, eyelet, cross and rococo stitches.

Opposite, right. South German whitework sampler on muslin. Rebekea Asch, 1758.

probably specifically for use as sampler cloth. It would be embroidered in silk. Towards the end of the 19th century, school samplers were done mostly on coarse canvas, although other samplers of the same period, which were probably made at home, were done on cotton cambric.

Early German samplers showed great restraint in the use of colour. But after the middle of the 19th century, the advent of aniline dyes brought a riot of colours (it was the Germans rather than the British who developed the manufacture of synthetic dyes from coal tar, and came more or less to monopolize the market). In Vierlande, a district on the Elbe near Hamburg, however, a characteristic style evolved, with black thread embroidery on linen, as in the beautiful, unfinished example shown.

Religious symbols appeared very frequently on 18th century German samplers, particularly on those from Protestant regions. In the 19th century, more worldly motifs came in: houses, town gates, village scenes, furniture, animals. One motif that never gained fashion was verse—religious or otherwise. There are small mottoes, usually of a religious tenor, but none of the endless exercises in lettering found in English samplers. Alphabets, however, were just as popular. They were not in the German script then in use, but in Roman or in beautiful, ornate Gothic.

German samplers were regarded as heirlooms. Those made by grandmother and mother were often kept together with that of the grand-daughter.

Many were framed, or kept lined with paper, or stretched over a board. One charming method was to finish off the sampler by mounting a silk ribbon around it, often ornamented with elaborate rosettes or ruching. This type of framing is also found in American samplers, and is obviously due to the influence of German settlers.

German sampler from Vierlande, 1741. Silk on fine linen worked mostly in cross and Gobelin stitches.

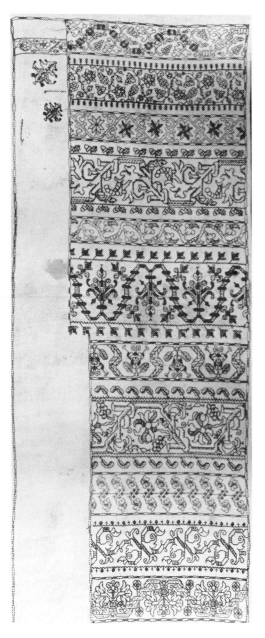

Above. Late 16th-century Italian blackwork sampler.

Italian sampler from near Perugia. Silk on linen. Worked in cross and eyelet stitches.

In Germany, the sampler remained a favourite needlework teaching method until after World War I. At that time the school curriculum was reorganised and the sampler was banned. After that, only students of textiles made samplers, for their own use. There is now, as in England and America, a revival of interest in samplers, both as collectable items and as a spare time activity.

In other European countries, too, sampler-making played an important part in women's lives. There was a constant interplay of ideas throughout Europe concerning designs and patterns, and this is clearly indicated in samplers. Each country, however, retained its own traditional treatment. Some of the motifs to be seen on British samplers of the late 17th century were copied from Dutch designs. Real Dutch samplers tended to be square or rectangular, and if the patterns showed great workmanship, the same designs were treated in England with a lighter touch and the shape of the samplers themselves was more varied. These influences are understandable, keeping in mind the close links established between the two countries when members of the English royal family spent years of exile in the Netherlands and even more when William of Orange became King of England. Darned samplers were as popular in Holland as they were in Germany.

In France, samplers do not seem to have held much popularity, judging by the scarcity of surviving specimens. The few that were made come from convent schools and show a high degree of proficiency. They were mostly religious in character, obviously a training before starting on ecclesiastical embroidery. French samplers are not generally pictorial and there is also an absence of verses. Very few workers recorded their age and the majority gave their initials rather than their name. There is much variety and subtlety in the use of emblems, floral designs and borders. These were often copied in England, and they can also be seen decorating 18th-century clothing.

Italian samplers showed graceful borders, colourful central work and geometrical designs of a floral type. The cut work and lace work of Italian

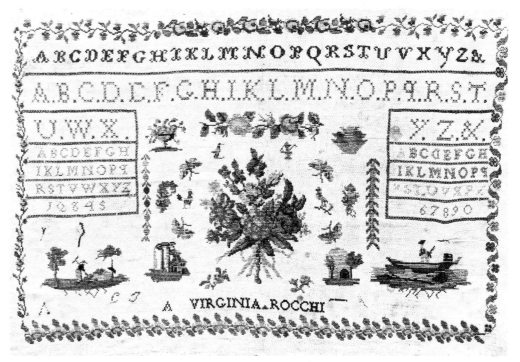

embroidery greatly influenced Britain and the rest of Europe in the 16th and 17th centuries.

Scandinavian samplers were done on fine muslin and show fine examples of drawn thread work. In Denmark, there was a time when only the nobility was allowed to wear lace. Ordinary women were incensed by this. They retaliated by evolving a type of embroidery that produced a lacy effect. This was originally made on cheese cloth and later on fine muslin, to be used on fichus and delicate blouses and aprons. The threads are not cut out, as in reticella, so the result is very strong, the threads of the fabric being merely pulled apart and reinforced by embroidery. A modern example of Scandinavian embroidery can be seen in Winifred Clayton's sampler.

Spanish and Mexican samplers were usually embroidered in silk, using bright colours. Drawn work was also popular, but by far the great majority of these samplers were done in cross-stitch. But to some extent this is true of any country, which is why cross-stitch is sometimes referred to as 'sampler stitch'.

Foreign samplers, just like their British counterparts, went through a slow

Spanish sampler worked in coloured silks on linen, 1756.

Danish pulled thread sampler worked by Winifred Clayton.

Mexican sampler, coloured silks on linen. Worked in satin stitch and drawn thread work, *c*1870.

process of decay from the middle of the 19th century. It was a natural death, as they seemed to have outlived their original purpose and had become stereotyped. Mary Eirween Jones argues that the Victorian sampler 'wilted because it lacked originality and aesthetic purpose.' 'To survive,' she writes, 'the sampler must adapt itself to the needs and ideas of the age in which it is worked.'

Mexican sampler in coloured silks and white cotton on linen. Worked in cross, Florentine, four-sided, back, straight, hem and pulled stitches. Hemmed edges, 1865. 15 × 34in.

Appendix 2 SAMPLER FABRICS

Homespun linen—the common clothing and household textile—was almost always used for 17th-century samplers. Occasionally, however, American samplers were made from cotton.

References from the 18th and 19th centuries describe catgut variously as a coarse and fine fabric, stiff enough to be used for lining and fine enough to be used for handkerchiefs and gauze dresses.

By the late 18th century, woollen bolting cloth or tammy was used. This was originally made for 'bolting' or sifting flour, but an inferior grade was produced in a special narrow width and known as 'sampler cloth'. It was widely used for the purpose, and is very commonly found in 19th century samplers. It is generally rather yellow, and is identifiable by a woven blue line in the selvage—and often, too, by the ravages of moths.

For the fine sort of samplers, the gauze-like fabric called tiffany was used. Darning samplers were generally worked upon it, because it shows the delicate woven patterns in silk to advantage. Usually, because it is transparent, it was lined with a coloured silk or satin. On American samplers the edges were bound or bordered round with silk ruffles.

Canvas or hempen cloth with spaced threads per inch became available from the 1840s. Cotton canvases from Germany were specially produced for Berlin work, as was the English Penelope canvas in which the threads were grouped in pairs. These threads could be separated so that both coarse and fine stitches could be worked on the same fabric.

To assist counting out the pattern the German canvas had a yellow thread every tenth square. The finest grade of canvas was called Silk or Mosaic. Later in the 19th century, thick canvases made in basket-weave pattern, with thick groups of threads and small spaced holes, were introduced. The linen sorts were known as Java, Aida, fancy oatmeal and Toile Colbert; the cotton variety was called Chessboard. The modern equivalent is Binca.

Crash has been used over a long period for embroidery, particularly English crewel work. It is a plain woven heavy linen or cotton, or a mixture of the two.

Glass cloths or good quality linen tea cloths were used, stripes and all, for 19th-century fancy work. These still make a reasonably cheap linen to work on.

Perhaps the most curious sampler material was a special sort of card available from the 1870s. Sheets were sold, usually in white, cream or gold, perforated all over with holes. These were frequently made into samplers by quite small children, using coloured wools, silks and beads. Worked moral texts and bookworks were also quite common. Contemporary encyclopaedias and magazines recommended binding the edges with ribbon to make three dimensional objects such as pin trays, letter racks, boxes and other fancy articles for bazaars.

Appendix 3 CLEANING METHODS

The cleaning of an old sampler must be carried out with great care as the effects will be irreversible and severe damage can result from the wrong cleaning method. Begin by vacuuming the sampler, as this will not cause any damage and will remove loose dust and dirt. The sampler should be placed flat under a piece of monofilament nylon net and vacuumed through it. The protective filament will hold the sampler in place and prevent strain on the delicate threads of the old fabric. The embroidered areas are usually far less likely to rip than the background linen.

If the sampler is very dirty or stained, washing may be the only solution. It is vital to test the embroidery for colour fastness. This entails testing each thread used in the embroidery as some colours may be fast and others not. It is sometimes possible to snip tiny scraps of loose thread from the back of the embroidery. They should be dampened and placed between two sheets of white blotting paper. If no discolouration appears on the paper, the sampler can be washed. It is a good idea to tack the sampler to a piece of plain cotton fabric or nylon netting before immersing it, as this will reduce tension on delicate fibres. Immerse flat—photographic developing trays are ideal—in lukewarm water containing Lissapol N*, a neutral detergent which is used in dilute solution. Do not rub or squeeze but sponge gently so that the water penetrates the fibres. Do not soak for long, but rinse thoroughly, using distilled water for the final rinse. Put the washed sampler on clean towels to catch the excess moisture. Straighten and smooth the sampler regularly. Once it is no longer dripping wet, it should be allowed to dry flat on a non-porous surface away from direct heat and strong light. If the sampler is embroidered on canvas, pin it on a block while it is still damp, as it may otherwise lose its shape or even shrink.

Once fully dry, the sampler can be delicately ironed from the wrong side using a damp cloth. Do not allow the iron to stand too heavily on the embroidery as this will flatten it or give it a matted look.

An old sampler may be damaged: moth holes in the embroidery can sometimes be quite invisibly darned if the right shade of thread can be found. Attach a small square of material under the hole and hold it in place with a few slip stitches done on the wrong side of the work, taking care that they do not show on the right side. Small areas of the embroidery can then be reconstituted. It is more difficult to cope with damage to the linen or woollen background cloth. It is better to leave these as they are and to mount the sampler on a piece of hardboard which has been covered with linen or cotton material in a colour which will blend with the sampler. Mount under glass, remembering to leave a small space between sampler and glass: a strip of acid-free card placed inside the frame will serve the purpose.

A modern sampler will be easier to wash, as modern embroidery threads tend to be colour fast. It can be washed in a mild detergent and, even if framed without a glass, will retain its freshness for years. Prevention being always better than cure, clean your unglazed sampler regularly with the upholstery attachment of a vacuum cleaner. Treated this way, your sampler should require washing only at very long intervals.

Hang the sampler, particularly if it is an old one, away from strong daylight and avoid steam and condensation. Fluorescent lamps should be filtered if they are used to illuminate the sampler as they emit ultra violet light which would fade the colours.

*Lissapol N can be obtained through Frank Joel, PO Box No. 6, Downham Market, Norfolk.

Suppliers

British Suppliers

Silken Threads (mail order only)
33 Linksway, Gatley, Cheadle, Cheshire, SK8 4LA
Artificial silk threads, twisted and floss
Chenille and fancy yarns
Tapestry wools
Transfer pencils
Needles

Russell & Chapple Ltd
23 Monmouth Street, London, WC2
Hessian

Luxury Needlepoint
36 Beauchamp Place, Brompton Road, London, SW3 1NU
Tapestry wool

Christine Riley
53 Barclay Street, Stonehaven, Kincardineshire, AB3 2AR
Embroidery threads, silks, cottons and wools
Canvas, linen and Hessian

The Handworkers Market
6 Bull Street, Holt, Norfolk
English, French tapestry and crewel wools
Stranded, twisted and soft cottons
Silks and floss
English, French and German canvas
Linen and cotton embroidery fabrics
Embroidery Frames

The Ladies Work Society Ltd
Delabere House, Moreton-in-Marsh, Gloucestershire
Crewel and tapestry wools
English, French and German Canvas

De Denne Ltd
159/161 Kenton Road, Kenton, Harrow, Middlesex
Embroidery materials and threads

The Silver Thimble
33 Gay Street, Bath, Avon, BA1 2NT
Tapestry, crewel and stranded wools
Stranded, twisted and soft cottons
Silk, linen thread.
Canvas, linen and cotton embroidery fabrics
Needles and embroidery frames

The Royal School of Needlework
25 Princes Gate, London, SW7 1QE
Canvas and linen
Crewel wools
Stranded and soft cottons
Needles and embroidery frames
Metal threads: including purl, bullion, passing and imitation Japanese gold

Heritage Crafts
76 Wey Hill, Haslemere, Surrey
Tapestry wools
Stranded, twisted and soft cottons
Embroidery linen and canvas

Mary Allen
Wirksworth, Derbyshire, DE4 4BN
Crewel and tapestry wools
Silk and cotton threads
Metallic threads
Linen and canvas

Mace & Nairn
89 Crane Street, Salisbury, Wiltshire, SP1 2PY
Silk and linen threads
Stranded twisted and soft cottons
Crewel and tapestry wools
Canvas, linen and cotton embroidery fabrics

Embroidery Art Supplies
56 Macauley Street, Grimsby, South Humberside
Embroidery frames

The Campden Needlecraft Centre
High Street, Chipping Campden, Gloucestershire
French and English embroidery wools and cottons
Canvas and linen

There are many excellent needlework shops throughout the United States. Below is a brief list of stores that will provide you with the raw materials for designing your own patterns if you do not have a favorite shop nearby.

California
The Needlecraft Shop
4501 Van Nuys Blvd., Sherman Oaks, Calif. 91403

Thumbelina Needlework Shop
1685 Copenhagen Dr., P.O. Box 1065, Solvang, Calif. 93463

Connecticut
The Hook 'N' Needle
1869 East State St., Westport, Conn. 06880

District of Columbia
The Elegant Needle
5430 MacArthur Blvd., N.W., Washington, D.C. 20016

Florida
Yarn and Design Studio
2156 Ponce de Leon Blvd., Coral Gables, Fla. 33134

Georgia
The Snail's Pace
548 E. Paces Ferry Rd., N.E., Atlanta, Ga. 30305

Massachusetts
The Crafts Centre
Quaker Road, Nantucket, Mass. 02554

The Stitchery
204 Worcester St., Wellesley Hills, Mass. 02181

Michigan
The Sampler
1011 S. Washington, Royal Oak, Mich. 48067

Minnesota
Stitch Niche
2866 Hennepin Ave., Minneapolis, Minn. 55408

Mississippi
Pandora's Box
P.O. Box E, Merigold, Miss. 38759

New Jersey
Janet's
Highway 35, Sea Girt, N.J. 08750

New York
The Open Door to Stitchery
4 Bond St., Great Neck, N.Y. 11021

Bell Yarn Co.
75 Essex St., N.Y., N.Y.

Alice Maynard
558 Madison Ave., N.Y., N.Y. 10022

Margot Gallery
26 W. 54th St., N.Y., N.Y. 10019

North Carolina
Ruth Leary's
382 N. Elm St., Greensboro, N.C. 27401

Oklahoma
The Yarn Garden, Inc.
10956 N. May Ave., Okla. City, Okla. 73120

Pennsylvania
Creative Stitchery
2116 Walnut St., Philadelphia, Pa. 19103

Texas
Deux Amis, Inc.
3708 Crawford, Austin, Tx. 78731

Virginia
Laura Weaver Needlework
Hotel Patrick Henry, 617 S. Jefferson St., Roanoke, Va. 24011

Washington
Phalice's Thread Web
W. 1301 14th Ave., Spokane, Wash. 99204

The following suppliers are good sources for all types of needlework materials. All of them are equipped to handle mail orders.

California
Dharma Trading Co.
P.O. Box 1288, Berkeley, Calif. 94701 (supplies include dyes)

Glen Black
1414 Grant Ave., San Francisco, Calif. 94133 (supplies include dyes)

Yarn Depot
545 Sutter St., San Francisco, Calif. 94102

Small Fortune
420 S. El Camino Real Tustin, Calif. 92680 (supplies include dyes)

Colorado
Countryside Handweavers, Inc.
West Elkhorn Ave., Box 1743, Estes Park, Colo. 80517

Connecticut
Yarn Primitives
Box 1013, Weston, Conn. 06880

Florida
Studio of Weaving and Lacemaking
319 Mendoza Ave., Coral Gables, Fla. 33134 (linen thread for lacemaking)

Illinois
Lee Wards
1200 St. Charles Rd., Elgin, Ill. 60120

Massachusetts
Nantucket Needleworks
11 South Water St., Nantucket, Mass.

Nantucket Needlery
2 India St., Nantucket, Mass. 02554

Michigan
Colonial Textiles
2604 Cranbrook, Ann Arbor, Mich. 48104

Old Mill Yarns
P.O. Box 115 WA, Eaton Rapids, Mich.

New Jersey
American Crewell and Canvas Studio
P.O. Box 1756, Point Pleasant Beach, N.J.

Judy's Originals
182 Mt. Bethel Rd., Warren, N.J.

New York
Paternayan Bros., Inc.
312 E. 95th St., N.Y., N.Y. 10028 (will inform you of outlets for their product in your locality)

Joan Toggitt
52 Vanderbilt Ave., N.Y., N.Y. 10017

North Carolina
Lily Mills
Shelby, N. Carolina (linen threads)

Rhode Island
Appleton Bros. of London
West Main Road, Little Compton, R.I. 02837

Craft Yarns of Rhode Island
603 Mineral Springs Ave., Pawtucket, R.I. 02862

Texas
Merribee
2904 W. Lancaster, Fort Worth, Tx. 76107

Manufacturers

Massachusetts
Frederick J. Fawcett, Inc.
129 South Street, Boston, Mass. 02111 (linen threads)

Needlecraft House
West Townsend, Massachusetts 01474 (yarns, canvas, needles)

New Jersey
The D.M.C. Corporation
107 Trumbull St., Elizabeth, N.J. 07206 (Retors à Broder, Mouliné, and cotton perlé, gold and silver metallic thread, canvas)

New York
Handwork Tapestries
Farmingdale, New York (French Toile Colbert and penelope canvas; all supplies for needlework canvas)

Brunswick Worsted Mills, Inc.
230 Fifth Ave., N.Y., N.Y. 10001 (wool orlan, mohair, angora yarns; canvas)

Bucilla Yarn Co.
230 Fifth Ave., N.Y., N.Y.

Columbia-Minerva
295 Fifth Ave., N.Y., N.Y. 10010 (yarn and canvas)

Paternayan Bros., inc.
312 E. 95th St., N.Y., N.Y. 10028 (Persian yarns; crewel, tapestry, and knitting yarns; needlepoint canvases; monk's cloth)

Tinsel Trading Co.
47 W. 38th St., N.Y., N.Y. (gold and silver lamé thread)

Joan Toggitt, Ltd.
246 Fifth Ave., N.Y., N.Y. (Marlitt and Bella Donna rayon thread, Pearsall silks, Knox's linen thread, canvas, wools, D.M.C. threads)

BIBLIOGRAPHY

Baker, Muriel and Lunt, Margaret. *Blue and White – The Cotton Embroideries of Rural China*. Charles Scribner & Sons (New York, 1977).

Beck, Thomasina. *Embroidered Gardens*. Angus & Robertson (London, 1979).

Blunt W. *The Art of Botanical Illustration*. Collins (London, 1950).

Bolton, Ethel Stanwood and Coe, Eva Johnston. *American Samplers*. National Society of the Colonial Dames of America: Massachusetts Branch (1921).

Brown, Harbeson Georgiana. *American Needlework: the history of stitchery from the late sixteenth to twentieth century*. Coward McCann (New York, 1938).

Campbell, Etha. *Linen Embroidery*. B.T. Batsford (London, 1957).

Caulfield, S.F. and Saward, B.C. *The Dictionary of Needlework*. L. Upcott Gill (London, 1921).

Christie, A. Grace I. *Samplers and Stitches*. B.T. Batsford (London, 1921).

Clucas, Joy. *Your Machine for Embroidery*. Bell & Hyman Ltd (London, 1973).

Dawson, Barbara. *Metal Thread Embroidery*. B.T. Batsford (London, 1968).

Dawson, Pam, *A Complete Guide to Embroidery*. Marshall Cavendish (London, 1972).

Digby, George Wingfield. *Elizabethan Embroidery*. Faber & Faber (London, 1963).

Dillmont, Thérèse de. *Encyclopedia of Needlework*. Editions T. de Dillmont (Paris, 1886).

Dreesman, Cécile. *Samplers for Today*. Van Nostrand Rheinhold (New York, 1972).

Drysdale, Rosemary. *The Art of Blackwork Embroidery*. Mills & Boon (London, 1975).

Finch, Karen and Putnam, Greta. *Caring for Textiles*. Barrie and Jenkins (London, 1977).

Geddes, E. and McNeill, M. *Blackwork Embroidery*. Dover reprint (New York, 1976).

Groves, Sylvia. *The History of Needlework Tools*. David & Charles (Newton Abbot, 1966).

Grow, Judith K. and McGrail, Elizabeth. *Creating history samplers*. Pyne Press (Princeton, 1974).

Hughes, Therle. *English Domestic Needlework*. Lutterworth Press (Guildford, 1961).

Huish, Marcus. *Samplers and Tapestry Embroideries*. Longmans & Co (London, 1900). Dover reprint (New York, 1970).

Jones, Mary Eirween. *A History of western Embroidery*. Studio Vista (London, 1969).

Kendrick, A.F. *English Needlework*. A & C Black (London, 1933).

King, Donald. *Samplers*. Victoria and Albert Museum (London, 1960).

Krueger, Glee. *A Gallery of American Samplers*. E.P. Dutton in association with the Museum of American Fold Art (New York, 1978).

Krueger, Glee. *New England Samplers to 1840*. Old Sturbridge Village (Sturbridge, Mass., 1978).

Lane, Rose Wilder. *Woman's Day Book of American Needlework*. B.T. Batsford (London, 1963).

Martin, Mary. *Mary Martin's Needlepoint*. William Morrow and Company, Inc. (New York, 1969).

Morris, Barbara. *Victorian Embroidery*. Herbert Jenkins (London, 1962).

Palliser, Fanny Bury. *A History of Lace*. Sampson Low & Co (London, 1875).

Schiffer, Margaret Berwind. *Historical Needlework of Pennsylvania*. Charles Scribner & Sons (New York, 1968).

Wade, N. Victoria. *The basic Stitches of Embroidery*. Victoria & Albert Museum (London, 1960).

Wardle, Patricia. *Guide to English Embroidery*. Victoria & Albert Museum (London, 1970).

White, A.V. *Blackwork Embroidery of Today*. Mills & Boon. (London, 1955).

Whiting, Gertrude. *Old-Time Tools and Toys of Needlework*. Dover Publications (New York, 1971).

INDEX OF STITCH DIAGRAMS

ACKNOWLEDGEMENTS

Photographers' names appear in brackets.

Reproduced by kind permission of Her Majesty the Queen: 14a, 21
Author's collection: 58d, 83c, 84, 86a & b, 88, 89, 94a, 97a, 131a, 132a
Blaise Castle Museum, Bristol: 55e, 86
The Bodleian Library, Oxford: 13b
Wm. Briggs & Co.: 94b
British Library (Ray Gardner): 22, 27a & b, 30b, 54a & c, 55d, 82a, 118, 119
The Brontë Society: 90b
Cambridge Folk Museum (Angelo Hornak): 58a
Ian Cameron: Title, Frontispiece, 125a, 126a & b, 127a,b,c, 128c, 129a & b, 130, 134, 151a
By kind permission of Sir John Carew-Pole, Bt. (Tom Molland): 18, 19a
Courtesy of the Cooper-Hewitt Museum, The Smithsonian Institution's National Museum of Design: 52b, 65a & b, 64, 69, 100, 104a,b,c, 105a & b, 150

Lillian Delevoryas: 124b
Embroiderers' Guild (Ian Cameron): 121, 124a, 128a, 131b
Mary Evans Picture Library: 81
Courtesy, Essex Institute, Salem, Massachusetts: 23, 63, 101, 102
Fitzwilliam Museum, Cambridge: 34
Mrs Nancy Fowler: 132c
Guildford Museum (Ian Cameron): 9, 32, 58b, 59, 60b, 82b, 83a, 85, 87a, 90a, 93, 97b, 120a, 123, 124a
Collection of Glee Krueger: 61, 68, 71, 103, 104d, 106
Leeds City Art Gallery, Temple Newsham House: 35a
The Mansell Collection: 11
Massachusetts Historical Society: 30a
The Metropolitan Museum of Art: Rogers Fund, 1913: 63
The Metropolitan Museum of Art: The Sylmaris Collection, Gift of George Coe Graves, 1930: 70
The Museum of London: 17b

National Portrait Gallery: 13a, 90c
By kind permission of The National Trust: Hardwick Hall: 15b
Pilgrim Society, Plymouth, Massachusetts: 66, 107
Pollock's Toy Museum: 58c
Bildarchiv Preussischer Kulturbesitz, Berlin: 147, 148
Private Collection: 12a
Mrs J. Quinson: 133
Ann Ronan Picture Library: 36
The Roosevelt Museum: 125b
Royal Scottish Museum, Edinburgh: 87b, 91, 99, 122, 151c
Tunbridge Wells Museum: 56, 83b, 92a, 98b
Victoria & Albert Museum: 14b, 15a, 17a, 20, 25a & b, 26, 28, 29, 31, 33b, 35b, 44, 46, 47, 52a, 54b, 55a,b,c, 60a, 95, 120b, 146a & b, 149a & b, 150, 151b
Welsh Folk Museum, St Fagans, Cardiff: 98a

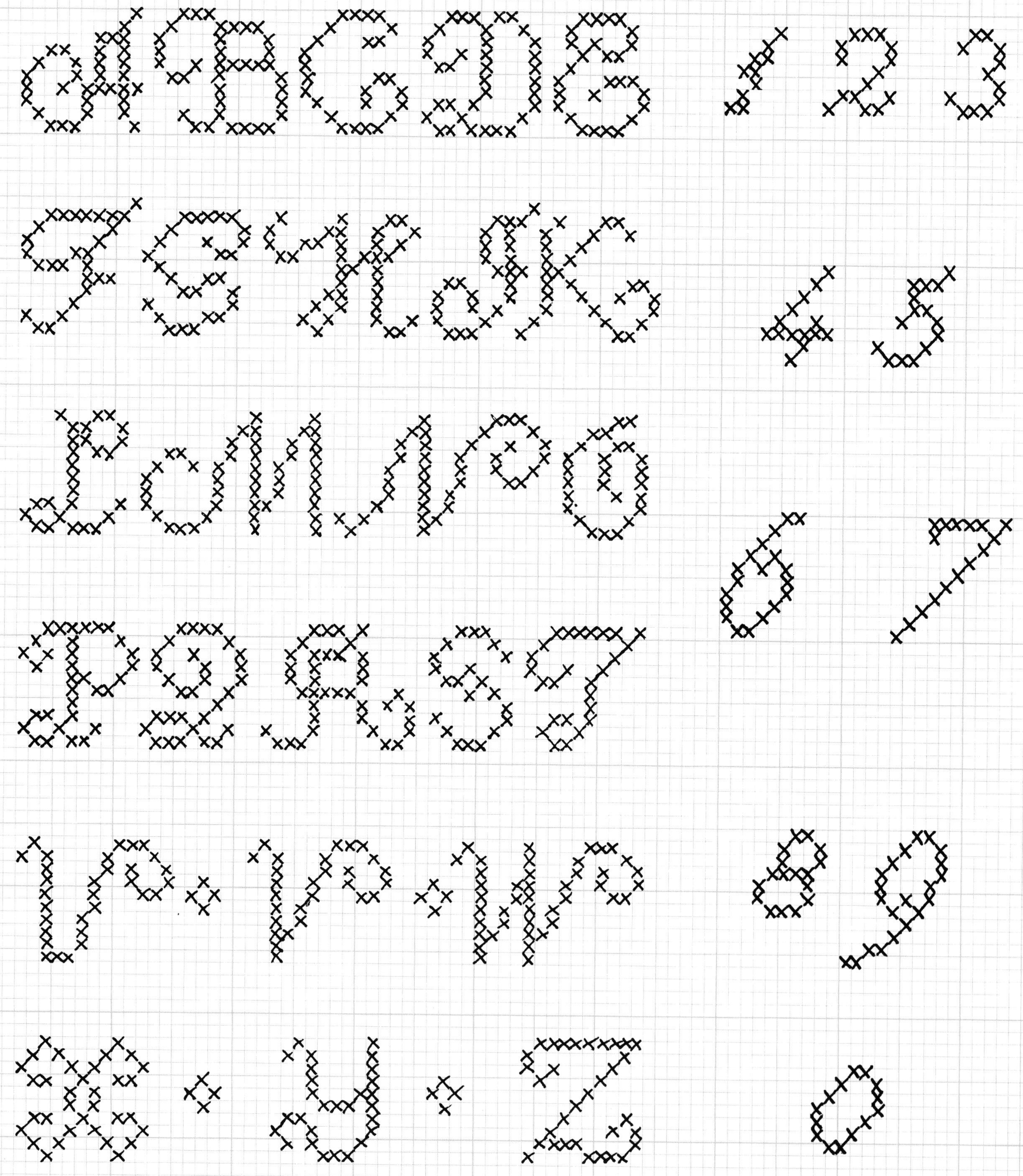

A B C D E 1 2 3

F G H I J K 4 5

L M N O 6 7

P Q R S T

U V W 8 9

X Y Z 0

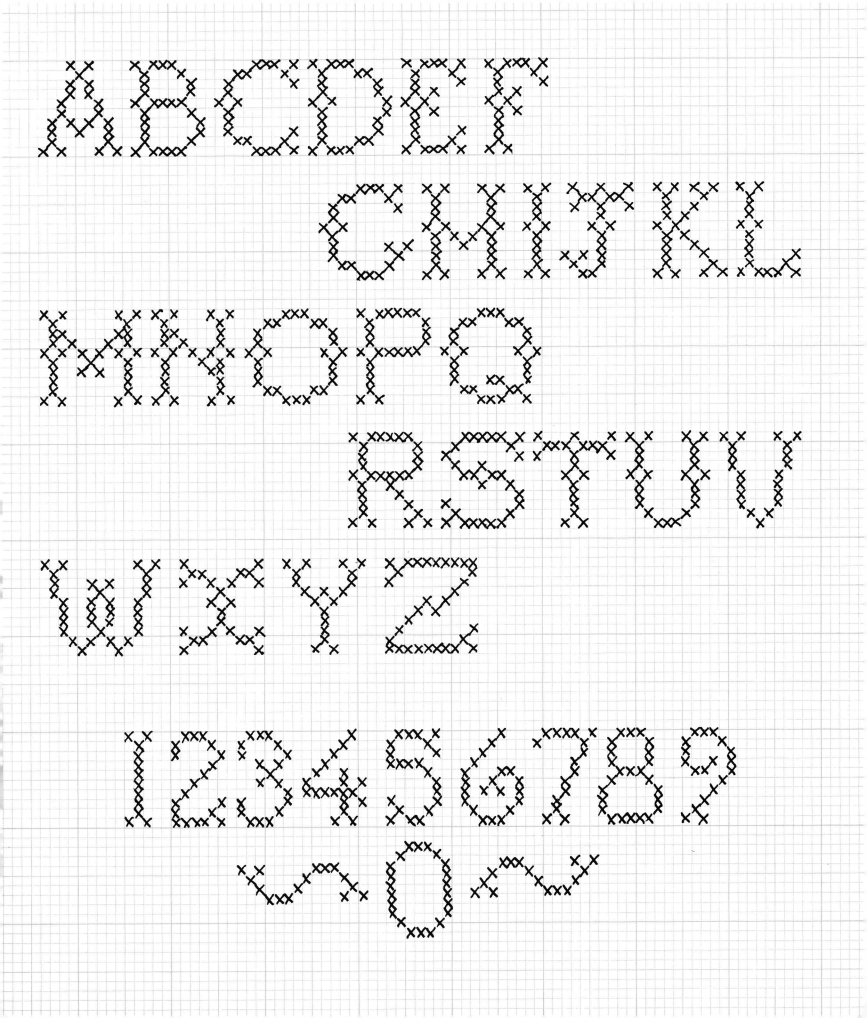

ABCDEF
GHIJKL
MNOPQ
RSTUV
WXYZ
123456789
0